Praise for How to Earn the Gift of Discretionary Effort

While at the most progressive steel maker in India several years ago the senior engineer gave me a tour of their operations during which we talked about management ideas, including their quality programs. He mentioned Quality Circles with what I saw as great pride. I stopped and pointed out that meant that everyone in a circle needed to be heard and respected. Did that mean destruction of the caste system?

He smiled beyond the normal confines of a mortal face, pumped his right hand and said "Yes!"

Since America's discovery of W. Edwards Deming's guidance to Japanese industry we have not only improved quality and reduced costs, we have changed society in profound ways. Through a steady accretion of insights about how to improve the delivery of goods and services we have moved from the human cogs of Henry Ford's assembly line to adding great value to the role individuals play in our businesses.

This steady advance has brought us to what I think is the next phase: understanding how to capture the immense power of the creative contributions of those who work with us.

And *How to Earn the Gift of Discretionary Effort* by Karla Brandau and Douglas Ross is the first big step toward that wonderful corporate condition.

– *Chris Cannon, thoughtful regulator (coal mine reclamation),*
industrialist (Geneva Steel) and congressman (R. UT 1997-2009)

How to Earn the Gift of Discretionary Effort is a novel and comprehensive approach to developing high-quality leadership skills. In this fast-developing and rapidly-changing business environment, such skills are absolutely essential to maintaining an edge over the competition. Ross and Brandau have tapped into the vast array of leadership characteristics to ferret out those qualities and techniques that best enable today/tomorrow's business and professional leaders become successful. This book is an absolute "must" for anyone aspiring to provide high-quality leadership to his/her organization.

   – Dr. Gerry Bissett, former Financial Services Senior Executive

***

Thank you for providing me your book, *How to Earn the Gift of Discretionary Effort*. It is a very thought-provoking treatise. I particularly appreciate that it is a practical checklist of leadership development practices supplemented with actual activities designed to habituate those practices.

   I hope to become a better leader by better engaging these practices, beginning with better expressions of gratitude for the great people I work with who do extend themselves in ways that are often under-appreciated and towards whom my appreciation is certainly under expressed.

   Thank you again.

   – Steve Lund, Chairman, Nu Skin Products

***

A man is judged by the company he keeps. A company is judged by the men (and women) they keep – the tragedy in today's companies is that half our work-force does not feel valued and what Brandau and Ross astutely recognize is that 'the first to leave are the productive ones who want to give their heart and head, not just their hands to their employers'. If you've wanted a manual for winning and keeping the hearts and minds of your employees, this is it.

   – Micheal Austin, Vice President, BYD

Brandau and Ross have raised the bar by clearly articulating the opportunities for principled leadership in corporate America. This is an inspirational and aspirational tome that states the case for opportunistic change while empowering leadership with the necessary tools to secure the gift of discretionary effort from the most important capital resource of any entity, its people.

The fundamental concept of 'the leadership of one' discussed by Brandau and Ross in this book is foundational to the core concept of 'earning the gift of discretionary effort'. The objective of any organization should be harnessing discretionary effort from its most important resource, its people. Brandau and Ross provide the needed tools to achieve such, and express this concept simply and effectively through the RossBrandau Leadership Model.

– David L. Parker, Partner, SRS Capital Partners

***

Weaving personal examples with dynamic principles, Brandau and Ross's work blueprints conditions for predictable reactions as influential to organizations as chemical reactions are to physical processes. Approaching discretionary effort as a gift to be earned injects a thoughtful juxtaposition worthy of a good read.

– William W. Maycock, Attorney at Law, Partner at Smith, Gambrell & Russell

***

How to Earn the Gift of Discretionary Effort focuses on qualities that are critical to building effective work environments and high performing teams. The use of practice steps at the end of each chapter allows you to reflect and embed these principles into your leadership style.

– Susan Keegan, Director of Advanced Analytics and Business Intelligence, Coca-Cola Enterprises

The book is intriguing. Visualizing the concepts of the book in creating a culture and environment of Discretionary Effort is inspiring.

– Lane R. Kofoed, President & CEO, Assisting Hands

***

There is nothing that substitutes for the horses. This mantra is what I live by every day in leading organizations through transformation. No product, no process, no leader can replace good people doing good things in your organization. Knowing that, I am always looking for ways to maximize the contribution from people...the horses.

How to Earn the Gift of Discretionary Effort, by Karla Brandau and Douglas Ross, is my new source for understanding more about the best kind of 21st century leadership. The basic tenets of leadership are found in myriad books, CDs, and podcasts but they typically focus on the nature of the employee e.g. what can leaders do to leverage, off-set, or even change the personality profile and work style of their people. But few resources teach leaders to focus on themselves--who also have unique personality profiles and work styles--such that the leaders become the catalysts for not only improved performance but increased capacity and contribution.

The gift of discretionary effort is just that...a gift. It can't be requisitioned or required, it comes to the organization after demonstrable efforts by its leaders to create an environment of trust, performance, autonomy, and accountability. I recommend a focused reading (or two) of this book and then the development of a plan for how you will use in your own organization--up the chain, down the chain, or both.

– Tim Germann, Founder, Principal Advisor, eXsilva Consulting

Whatever your "leadership style," whatever leadership theories you subscribe to, the bottom line is productivity. How do you get people to do what they need to do, consistently and to the best of their ability—for their own sake as well as the organization's? The secret, as Brandau and Ross reveal, is discretionary effort. This book explains how you can earn that kind of effort from those you lead on a daily basis, by practicing the principles of authentic, compassionate leadership. Well written and engaging, *How to Earn the Gift of Discretionary Effort* is required reading for organizational leaders at every level.

> – *Rob Jenkins, 30-year veteran of higher education and author of The 9 Virtues of Exceptional Leaders*

***

I only wish this book were available 20 years ago when I was starting my business. Brandau and Ross have opened my eyes to the idea that discretionary effort is what distinguishes star employees from the rest. This essential hands-on book coaches leaders to realize the best from their organizations.

> – *Lisa Sorensen, President, Sisters' Gourmet, Inc.*

How To Earn The

Gift

Of DISCRETIONARY EFFORT

by KARLA BRANDAU and DOUGLAS ROSS

How to Earn the Gift of Discretionary Effort

Edited by Kiffany Javier

Book and cover design by Rebecca Hayes

Published in the United States by
Life Power Publishing

ISBN-13: 978-1-892968-11-1

Dedication

To Steve who has been supportive through thick and thin and has kept us steadily moving forward. He has been the wind beneath our wings.

Acknowledgements

Doug and Karla acknowledge the tremendous contributions of these people:

Kiffany Javier who edited the finished copy with deftness and precision.

Rebecca Hayes for her flare for design. She did the book cover, formatting, and graphic design.

Dave DiMartile, Richard Snary and Bill Shaw for the foundational thinking on discretionary effort they shared with us.

Contents

INTRODUCTION

New Leadership Strategies for the 21st Century

"Given the fact that we are in a capitalist society, we still do not want to overlook not only what a corporation produces and its profitability but also how it impacts the environment, touches human life and whether it protects or undermines the dignity of the human soul."
~ Dean Smith

Wake Up Call

Great leaders do not sugar coat the truth. When the past recession hit, one CEO of a large manufacturing company confronted the realities and knew something had to change for his company to survive. Peering over his reading glasses, he looked across the desk at one of his employees and said, "Nothing in this company is sacred. Everything will be evaluated and put on the chopping block in order to maintain profitability. This economy is but a wake-up call. We will survive."

Leadership teams across the world hear the wake-up call whenever an economic recession hits, but the quickly changing landscape of the 21st century requires continuous refocus to survive as an organization. The constant evaluation of organizational performance includes leadership practices.

The most recent worldwide economic downturn was not a mere fluctuation in the market, but was revolutionary, causing seismic shifts in business procedures and in organizational social structures that affect profitability, economic sustainability, and discretionary effort. The recession caused organizations to look at the principles that guide their leadership teams to enable them to better navigate the complexity of their workplace culture amid the uncertainties of the global economic environment.

Outdated People Practices

A current deterioration of business results may be attributed to changing market conditions or to the inability to compete with the improved products and services offered by competitors. These may be factors in such a complex issue as market success, but we maintain the real culprit is failure to create an environment where discretionary effort is freely given by every employee on a daily basis.

As your leadership team evaluates your people practices that discourage discretionary effort, you may observe that some practices are outdated because they were designed from the implicit social contracts of the 20th century. While these people policies worked at one time, most of them are declining in their effectiveness, especially with the new workers entering the workforce.

One of the 20th century declining people philosophies is "do more with less." Companies under pressure to improve revenues let people go and put extreme stress on machinery, supply chains, and workers to produce the maximum in the shortest time with the fewest resources.

The practice of pushing people to work harder and faster is a temporary solution that more than enough employees are willing to deliver when occasionally asked. However, if the organization asks for the same maximized effort every week, there are consequences. Workers become tired and make mistakes. Their home lives become unbalanced, and employees' families can experience resentment. Employees could be asked to temporarily overlook safety or quality procedures that are necessary for product integrity but not overtly noticeable to a customer. What if, however, while temporarily overlooking safety or quality, a severe problem surfaces with the product or an employee gets seriously hurt at work?

A problem with the do-more-with-less approach is that it assumes increased demand can be met simply by squeezing more out of the system. The hidden reality is that every system has built-in inefficiencies, and when leadership teams start looking to reduce wastefulness and ineffectiveness, they set countless improvements in motion.

21st Century People Practices

Simultaneously with the discovery and elimination of inefficiencies, leaders can start the process of establishing a culture that earns the gift of discretionary effort on a regular basis. Discretionary effort is the key to 21st century productivity and economic sustainability. The gift of discretionary effort is built on valuing human dignity, creating safety and security, extending social acceptance, and rationally aligning each individual employee with company purposes.

    This book discusses the implementation of these strategies.

CHAPTER 1

The Discretionary Effort Leadership Model

"A leader is one who knows the way, goes the way,
and shows the way."
~ *John C. Maxwell*

This book examines your company's people policies and guides you to create an organizational culture that enables employees to release their gifts of discretionary effort on a regular basis. This is accomplished by the implementation of the RossBrandau Discretionary Effort Leadership Model. Before introducing and coaching you through the implementation of the model, let's clarify the phrase discretionary effort.

What is Discretionary Effort?

Cultivating discretionary effort is both an individual and a collective process to improve the level of energy and innovation that flows within an organization. It is neither a quick fix nor an expensive, resource-depleting process, and when done in a measured and incremental way, discretionary effort is a breakthrough improvement.

> Discretionary effort is the amount of effort workers are capable of bringing to an activity versus what they have to do to get a pay check.

Traditional literature defines discretionary effort as the difference between the level of effort a worker is *capable* of bringing to an activity or task and the *minimum effort required* to do the work and get a pay check. This minimum level of effort can be made by employees who are competent at their jobs but who are relatively unengaged in the overall goals of the company.

For example, experienced and knowledgeable workers may only be giving the minimum level of effort as they do routine work required by their job description: processing invoices, making sales calls, writing proposals, etc. How would the results of their work be different if they understood the goals of the company and were giving discretionary effort instead of the minimum required to keep their job?

> Giving discretionary effort is a voluntary and free-will choice each employee makes.

Giving discretionary effort is a voluntary act. When an employee gives the company discretionary effort, it is an intentional, free-will choice. Before discretionary effort contributions are observable, they exist as potential in the mind of every employee as ideas to improve what is happening. These ideas represent great power waiting to be tapped; power that increase resources and reduce costs as workers add value to the tasks they perform. With a limited awareness, leadership teams often think doing more with less is about computers, technology, and waste reduction strategies. Doing more with less includes this hidden gem of teaching managers how to earn the gift of discretionary effort from employees as opposed to demanding or forcing extra effort and long hours.

What Does It Mean to Earn the Gift?

Every employee has gifts or talents that are not visible on a resume or in a hiring interview. Some of these are gifts of character such as determination, purpose, and resilience. Think of the talents of employees wrapped in beautiful boxes sitting around them on the floor and on their desks. With this analogy, your entire office building would be filled with impressively wrapped packages waiting to be unwrapped as if it were a birthday party where the "gifts" are regularly unwrapped. The workers give these packages to you and their coworkers as your leadership team works with the concepts in this book and implements the RossBrandau Leadership Model.

Earning the gift of discretionary effort from employees begins with the members of your leadership team living and breathing the five levels of our leadership model themselves. As the leaders practice integrity and unwrap their own gifts of discretionary effort, their direct reports will see the positive results and want to imitate the leaders' examples. In an environment of mutual confidence and trust, managers are respected and are in a position to earn the gifts of discretionary effort from employees. When discretionary effort is displayed by management and is engrained in the culture, workers freely unwrap their gifts of discretionary effort as needed because they feel safe, respected, and trusted.

A man at one company where we consulted told us, "My company has had my hands for over 30 years. You know, they could have had my head as well." This quote illustrates two things. First, some companies do not place appropriate value on the gifts of the individual employee. Second, most workers want to contribute at higher levels than their environments allow. Discretionary effort is earned by recognizing workers as resources that can bring value beyond the obvious academic discipline and skills for which they were hired.

The RossBrandau Leadership Model helps leaders earn the gift of discretionary effort and the release of knowledge that resides in the brains of employees on a daily basis, both of which help the company move forward to increased economic sustainability.

What is the RossBrandau Leadership Model?

Figure 1.1 summarizes the RossBrandau Leadership Model and the conditions that invite discretionary effort in the workplace.

When implemented, the five levels outlined in the model make it possible for leaders at all ranks of the organization to earn the gift of discretionary effort from employees on a regular basis. Notice that a work environment of integrity and gratitude provides a solid foundation for the implementation of the five levels. Integrity and gratitude are discussed in Chapters 2 and 3. Built upon the proper foundation, it is possible to then establish the five levels of the RossBrandau Leadership Model:

RossBrandau Discretionary Effort Leadership Model

PROFITABILITY AND ECONOMIC SUSTAINABILITY

Authentic Contribution

Emotional Commitment

Rational Alignment

Social Acceptance

Safety and Security

WORK ENVIRONMENT OF INTEGRITY AND GRATITUDE

Figure 1.1: The five levels of the leadership model

1. **Safety and Security.** Leadership Level 1 provides a safe and secure working environment for employees. Rules are followed, validated, improved, refined, and recognized on a daily basis at an individual level throughout the organization. Employers place high worth on the security of every worker. The focus on security provides an environment free from bodily harm. A safe and secure environment is essential in order for

employees to concentrate on continuous improvement. Employees need to be free to work rather than worry about safety and security issues.

2. **Social Acceptance.** Leadership Level 2 describes the cultural norms and behaviors that recognize the human dignity of all employees. Everyone is recognized as a value-added part of the whole, or part of the family. Employees want to feel they are part of the core group. The more they feel part of the whole team, the more success will develop as they voluntarily contribute their discretionary energy.

3. **Rational Alignment.** Leadership Level 3 is critical to the functioning of the entire organization. It is here that values, vision, and mission statements flow into long-term objectives and deadlines. Employees logically align with the values, vision, and mission of the organization and then rationally make daily work plans to reflect their stewardship. The daily tasks must rationally align with work output needed to move projects from theory into reality.

At this point in the process, it is important to assess the company systems, policies, and procedures to ensure the first three levels are not being inadvertently sabotaged. If the company is structurally sound and the first three levels are carefully implemented, the fourth and fifth levels will happen naturally.

4. **Emotional Commitment.** Leadership Level 4 describes the difference between engagement and emotional commitment. Manifestations of low emotional commitment hinder and impede the flow of discretionary effort individually and collectively. Exhibiting emotional commitment clears the way for objective, value-added solutions where employees collaborate to solve complex problems and communicate to overcome misunderstandings.

5. **Authentic Contribution.** The entire organization will recognize a victory when employees move to Leadership Level 5. At this level, all team members

take ownership and treat the business as their own. Employees take on the feel of partners in the organization.

Understanding how these five levels work is the key to organizational profitability and economic sustainability.

The Growth of Discretionary Effort

Figure 1.2: Predictable behaviors within the five levels of the leadership model

As your leadership team develops their competencies in these five levels, they will see predictable employee behaviors that correspond to each leadership level as shown in Figure 1.2. We identify several predictable employee behaviors:

Conforming. At Leadership Level 1, Security and Well-Being, employees will conform to rules and regulations to ensure the security of the workplace for every employee. Compliance to certain safety standards is mandatory.

Relating. In Leadership Level 2, Social Acceptance, employees will be interacting with each other and building strong professional relationships. Conversations will be genuine and people will be able to successfully negotiate differences of opinions while finding solutions to problems.

Aligning. With Leadership Level 3, Rational Alignment, employees actively and willingly align with the purpose of the organization and give the organization discretionary effort and intellectual mindshare. They align their daily activities with the goals and objectives of the company.

Supporting. In Leadership Level 4, Emotional Commitment, employees will demonstrate they have bought in by actively working together to move projects forward on a timely basis. They mentally and emotionally support company initiatives and can work collaboratively with each other.

Leading. When employees reach Leadership Level 5, Authentic Contribution, employees lead regardless of their place on the organizational chart. When they have expertise, they lead. The leadership team encourages this as it accepts that employees are subject matter experts in the areas they control and are capable of providing value added leadership.

In summary, your leadership teams will have unimaginable influence if they understand the power of these simple but essential leadership levels. They will become leaders who:

- Can be trusted whether in a difficult present or an ambiguous future
- Have laser focus on creating alignment of objectives and processes
- Understand the collaborative problem-solving process
- Are willing to let go of control in order to establish shared accountability
- Care about employees as human beings

These qualities make it possible for your leadership team to create a culture where employees are engaged and support organizational objectives, collaborate with each other, and give discretionary effort. These are necessary behaviors in order for your company to create profits and maintain economic sustainability.

Transforming to a Human-led Value Culture

The move toward earning the gift of discretionary effort by using 21st century people-policies requires transforming the company philosophy to a human-led value culture. For many organizations, this is a game-changer and a split from an operational-based system. In an operational-led value system, management's highest priority is designing business systems and controlling the process of production for the highest output of goods and services in a certain amount of time. As we discuss in Chapter 7, the operational-based system is a 20th century strategy. A human-led value culture changes the focus to people policies that allow organizational objectives to be met by employees who give their personal best–or as we term it, voluntarily give discretionary effort.

> The practice of giving discretionary effort requires perseverance until it becomes part of the company culture.

Understanding human worth and implementing policies where individuals flourish help companies maintain economic stability and weather recessions and market downturns. A human-led value culture is built on trust, integrity, and gratitude. It is a culture that permits employees to enter the conversation and be heard on issues that affect them. A basic principle in a human-led value culture is that taking care of employees is taking care of business.

An American Psychological Association (APA) survey conducted in 2011 found that only 52 percent of employees said they feel valued on the job and motivated to do their best work. What would happen to productivity if by using the RossBrandau Leadership Model, that percentage of employees could be increased? We believe the company would see significant improvements in productivity and morale.

Implementing a human-led value culture "keeps the grass watered on your side of the fence."

Top level employees stay because they are moved from merely earning a pay check to feeling valued for their skills, talents, character gifts, and ideas they interject into corporate conversations. If an engaging work environment that recognizes the worth of individuals is not created in the company, the

> If the leadership team fails in creating an engaging work environment, the weak performers are not the first to leave.

weak performers are not the first to leave. The first to leave are the productive ones who want to give their heart and head, not just their hands to their employer. This makes the implementation of the RossBrandau Leadership Model and a human-led value culture part of the formula for employee retention which is more reliable than traditional pension plans and promises of post-retirement healthcare, both of which retain less motivated personnel.

When capable employees work in a human-led company culture created by the RossBrandau Model, they are more committed to the company's mission and goals.

The Role of the Leadership Team

To release the gift of discretionary effort inside every employee is the challenge of leadership teams. This requires consistency, continual effort, and perseverance on the part of the leadership team until it becomes part of an organization's best practices. When it becomes part of the culture, it quickly becomes a performance improvement strategy when a few dedicated employees exhibit discretionary effort, coworkers observe their efforts and tend to increase their own efforts, creating an invigorating effect throughout the entire organization.

In his article, "The Law of Accelerating Returns," Ray Kurzweil (2001), American scientist and futurist, says: "Technological change is exponential, contrary to the common-sense 'intuitive linear' view. So we won't experience 100 years of progress in the 21st century—it will be more like 20,000 years of progress (at today's rate)."

Leadership teams simply cannot keep up with this pace of change without the assistance of workers who are engaged in giving discretionary effort and who willingly share their creative ideas in collaborative ways. According to the majority of reports that have been recently written, new generations of employees want to be engaged in their work and feel that what they are contributing matters. They will give their hearts and heads, not just their hands, to a company that lives the RossBrandau Leadership Model. Organizations that implement our model will be targeted by top talent from other companies as an organization they want to join.

One employee who wanted to contribute at the heart and head level had idea for a new product line that was first rejected by his direct managers because they thought it would not enhance the brand image. After consideration, they gave him permission to try the idea if it didn't conflict with getting his assigned work completed. This employee formed a volunteer team with two other employees to see if the concept worked. After hours the team put together a prototype product with rejected parts.

The next time the corporate CEO was on site, the volunteer team asked him if he wanted to look at a little skunkworks project. The CEO loved the prototype and that product became an integral part of the company's branding as its highest selling and most profitable product. The skunkworks project cost the organization nothing. It was a product of discretionary effort.

Not every act of discretionary effort results in a new product. Many acts of discretionary effort positively impact the operation without any fanfare. However, it is a leader's responsibility to take the time to see and recognize overlooked actions, the gifts of discretionary effort the employee gives. Every time a leader acknowledges one small act, the relationship between the employee and the manager is enhanced. If the acknowledgment is witnessed by other employees, they, too, seek recognition and begin contributing in their own ways. This is the multiplier effect which we will discuss in more detail in a later chapter.

Once leaders become curious about discretionary effort and make a conscious endeavor to look for it, they will notice it everywhere. The essential contributions given by regular, everyday people doing ordinary jobs will be apparent at all levels of the organization. As their contributions are acknowledged, company growth is pushed forward by everyone, not just a few employees.

Understanding Authentic Leadership - the Leadership of One

A key element of the implementation of the RossBrandau Leadership Model could go by many different names: self-leadership, self-less leadership, leadership by example, or personal leadership. We call it the "Leadership of One," and it is incumbent on every member of the leadership team to become an authentic leader.

This term, the Leadership of One, came from a regional director of a multinational company. The director asked his senior team to prepare for an upcoming meeting by identifying the major challenge they were facing as an organization.

The team spent many days contemplating the question and formulating responses and action plans. In preparation for the upcoming meeting, the director was asked by one of his direct reports for clarification. The director merely said, "The major challenge we have is leadership." He continued to explain that the organization was not realizing the possibilities they had set forth in their goals for performance, so the issue was within their leadership team. "We have incredible hand, heart, and mind resources that we are not tapping into," he explained.

When this information was relayed back to members of the team, each one confided and said in different ways: "I wonder which person he is trying to move out of the organization." In essence, each of them said, "It is not me; I wonder who is not leading his or her area properly."

It was evident what the director was alluding to. Unless the team members could admit they were part of the problem, the entire organization would continue to suffer. Each individual needed to evaluate his or her leadership practices that might be blocking attainment of the company goals.

During the unforgettable meeting, the managers stood up one by one and clearly articulated what they thought the problem was and what they were going to do. For the most part, the plans were developed within their individual silos. The entire management team considered each plan, discussing points in support of the issues identified. The director listened politely to everything and said nothing.

At the end of the meeting, the director acknowledged everyone for identifying what they thought was the issue and the aggressive actions they planned to take. He complimented the team members on being honest and forthright about their perspectives on other's challenges and plans. He then said, "I have not heard what I think is the real issue." He continued, "We have a leadership issue. Each one of you has only *one person to lead*. If you individually can't get to this challenge and we collectively don't have the willingness to face it, then we will continue to get the same performance we have always gotten."

"You have only one person to lead." What did the regional director mean? The lesson taken from his words that applies to discretionary effort is, unless you can tap into your own energy and unwrap your gifts of discretionary effort on a daily basis, you cannot legislate, demand, or manage the potential effort your employees have to offer. This involves learning and growing as a leader. In essence, you have to walk it before you can talk it. As giving discretionary effort and energy becomes habitual for you, it provides an example for employees of personal excellence. Conscientious individuals will follow your lead.

The Leadership of One Analogy

You have only one person to lead.

LEADERSHIP OF ONE
POWERFUL PRINCIPLE

In every chapter of this book, you will see a picture of a fish along with a specific focal point for our philosophy about becoming a leader people choose to follow. We have written a book entitled, *The Leadership of One* (2016) that explains the philosophy. The fish is a fitting symbol of our philosophy because of fish behaviors which include swimming in synchronicity, shoaling, and one fish taking the lead.

Swimming in synchronicity. A group of fish swimming together as if they were performing a water ballet is called a school of fish. They swim in a synchronized fashion, moving in the same direction, at the same speed, and turning simultaneously. To have all employees on point, moving in the same direction toward goals and objectives is the goal of company leadership teams.

Shoaling. However, most employees are not synchronized, they are in a social group. In fish, biologists term social swimming as "shoaling." When fish shoal, they stay together, but they perform and move independently. Shoaling helps fish to forage for food and protect themselves from predators, but it is not an effective way to move to a desired location. Similarly, shoaling gives teams in companies the benefits of a social group, but it is not the most effective way to achieve a desired goal.

Being mindful of others. How do fish, spread over a considerable distance, coordinate their swimming to be precisely together? Biologists have found they keep an eye on their immediate neighbors. Teaching team members to look out for one another's security, or to "have each other's back" while swimming toward the objective are the how-to principles we teach in *The Leadership of One.* As team members accept the strengths and limitations of their peers and learn to swim in a synchronized fashion, they reach their objectives of economic stability and keep marketplace predators at bay.

Directionless synchronicity. Despite swimming precisely together, looking as if they are aligned in all aspects of life, a school of fish is basically directionless. They swim at the whim of a fish that wants to change direction or perceives a predator. As one darts in a new direction, all fish in the school follow.

One gold fish takes the lead. Just as one fish can turn the entire group, one enlightened person can lead the team and the entire company in new directions. For this to happen, the person must have a vision and the skills to communicate that vision in an authentic way. As individuals perceive a new direction and practice discretionary effort by adding creative problem-solving ideas to the discussion, they stop following and start leading in a new direction.

With their leadership skills, they become the "golden fish" people *choose* to follow, not *have* to follow.

Discretionary Effort Exercise Overview and Instruction

The practice of discretionary effort involves taking ownership of what you learn and practicing it in a variety of new situations, permitting you to internalize the concept. For this purpose, at the end of each chapter is a 21st century Leadership of One Power Principle. This is followed by a reflection section that summarizes the chapter and discusses the rationale and objectives of the principle. Next, a discretionary effort exercise fosters the leadership principle at work. This exercise is built on a concept called praxis, which means being practical with an end goal of action, not theory.

Praxis is a unique contribution to the general theory of neuroplasticity. Neuroplasticity simply states that your brain has the ability to change itself. The challenge is to find new ways to stimulate the ability to change. New learning is at the heart of the brain's ability to change itself and is stimulated by real world challenges that block or inhibit the habitual behaviors. The research into neuroplasticity has up to this point focused on learning how the brain reprograms itself after strokes that resulted in physical impairment, but it has applications for anyone who wants to learn and improve.

The challenge of discretionary effort is not physical but rather mental, emotional, and rational. The purpose of the practice process is to find a solution to disagreements and problems that is more productive and workable than the one currently being used. Individuals who embrace the discretionary effort challenge engage in activities that create new learning and the development of new, productive and sustainable behaviors.

In the interest of efficiency and effectiveness, the brain creates channels to process information that result in automatic actions which we typically call habits. Habits help when you walk into an experience that is somewhat familiar. You can react in a habitual way, saving the time and effort of figuring out a new way of responding. Habitual responses become an automatic command.

Habits are hurtful when automatic commands do not work in the new situations or conversations we encounter in a complex workday. You can tell because tempers flare, people shut down, and communication stops. It is important to recognize that our habitual way of responding is counterproductive. Now is the time to create new learning by pausing, evaluating the situation, and working to see the situation differently, thus creating a new experience.

Now the brain can change itself as the new experience creates new neural pathways. These new routes made of inter-communicating neurons are not habits or skills yet. These routes can be compared to lenses in the eye which translate what we see for the brain to understand. The new neural pathways only become habits that improve your functioning through learning and repetition, much like a mountain path is created through daily use by a shepherd and his herd.

The unique contribution of the practice of discretionary effort to the field of neuroplasticity is the creation of statements that force you outside of your normal ways of seeing and interpreting reality. For example, the statement you will practice in this chapter is "You only have one person to lead."

While performing daily activities, simply repeating the statement "You only have one person to lead" pushes you down the path of creating better automatic responses. The purpose is to train the brain to look at new and out-of-the ordinary things that are happening all around but have become invisible to you. The statement intentionally disrupts your ordinary way of responding, while the stimulation of new neural pathways opens fresh, creative ways of seeing and processing information.

Discretionary Effort Practice Steps

At the end of each chapter, there are practice steps designed to help you incorporate what is learned intellectually into actions in your daily routines. These steps are practical exercises but the statements only become powerful change agents when contemplated and impressions acted on. In essence, the exercises ask you to see things differently, create a fresh viewpoint, and learn new ways of responding that will advance a 21st century leadership culture in your organization. The tasks become the vehicle to releasing the gift of discretionary effort within yourself first and then within the organization.

Completing the practices utilizes the "Kata" discipline. Kata is a Japanese word coming from karate and other martial art forms. It is a structured routine practiced deliberately in order to create new habits (Rother 2010). As an example, getting into a new car for the first time is the beginning of the Kata practice. The driver positions the seat to be the right distance from the pedal, figures out how to fasten the seat belt and how to start the car. Next, the driver explores how to turn on the heat or air conditioner, finds a music station, and adjusts the side and front mirrors for safety.

This is a routine you have practiced every day until it is an automatic response. When you get into a rental car, you are slightly disorientated, but you fall back on your automatic routine, make a few adjustments, and drive off. It is the same with discretionary effort; you develop a practice routine that releases the energy of discretionary effort until it becomes automatic.

In the martial arts, the goal of Kata, or the practice of form and repetitive actions, is to make proven techniques of self-defense automatic. This is illustrated in the "wax on, wax off" exercise made popular in *The Karate Kid* movie. Applying Kata to the development of discretionary effort means practicing in a repetitive manner the skills and abilities needed to build credibility, integrity, and superior relationships on a daily basis.

In order to apply and practice the principles of each chapter, you will be asked to contemplate a statement for one week. At the end of a week, you will ask yourself four questions. The first question asks you to evaluate the breakthroughs and the possible breakdowns associated with the statement. A breakthrough is an important discovery. A breakdown is an occurrence or failure that prevented completion of a task or success. The other two questions deal with introspection and future application of the principle.

This pattern is illustrated below and will follow at the end of each chapter.

The Practice of Discretionary Effort

Leadership of One Power Principle: Be the leader people choose to follow by recognizing you only have one person to lead.

Reflection

Implementing the RossBrandau Leadership Model requires understanding the meaning of "you only have one person to lead." When personal character and people skills are expanded through personal development, you are in effect leading yourself. Those you interface with every day will observe improved success when reacting to difficult situations and complex circumstances. They will want to emulate your effectiveness.

Leading yourself is a journey to become a more effective leader. You will gain the ability to evaluate your daily reactions to difficult situations and determine if you made the best behavior choice. The personal development found when following the Leadership of One Power Principles will help you improve your reactions to difficult situations. As your behaviors mold new ways of interacting, people will follow you by choice.

Discretionary Effort Exercise:

I Have Only One Person To Lead

The exercise for this chapter is to discover how to begin to lead yourself from inner confusion to the discovery and refinement of your own unique gifts and talents. This allows you to display the skills and abilities of a leader that people admire and want to emulate. As you go about your daily routines repeat the word "I only have one person to lead." When you do this, your mind begins to see and then react to things differently. It creates new pathways in your brain.

Most people are not used to thinking about how to lead themselves as management literature and coaching focuses on how to lead others, yet thousands of times a day we evaluate, judge, and act very quickly with automatic responses that usually give us the same outcomes we had previously. If the outcomes of your automatic responses are good, continue. If they are questionable, rethink and try the strategies suggested in the Power Principles and the RossBrandau Leadership Model. You may have heard Albert Einstein's definition of insanity: doing the same thing and expecting a different outcome. Avoid insanity.

The saying "you only have one person to lead" is designed to bring to your awareness automatic responses, help you evaluate what's effective, and decide if you want to choose another way of responding. The next time you are in the presence of colleagues, team members, or your direct reports and are faced with a decision to evaluate and act on, remind yourself "I only have one person to lead" and assess how you might look at the situation differently. By changing and improving your reactions, you steadily move toward the leader people choose to follow because they see a better path.

Discretionary Effort Practice Steps

Step 1: Observe and Experience. In the course of your day look for examples of how you lead yourself or how your automatic responses lead you to the same outcome of your prior encounter. Look at how others also lead themselves and observe the outcomes they get.

Step 2: Contemplate and Record. Maintain a record of your observations of the how you lead yourself and how others lead themselves.

Step 3: Share, Learn, and Model. After you have evaluated the following questions, share your insights and ask for input from a mentor, a friend, or trusted advisor.

What personal breakthroughs did I have in discovering my way of leading? Did I observe any breakdowns in my leadership—did I inadvertently have the same outcome as in a previous encounter or circumstance?

What breakthroughs or breakdowns did I observe about the way others lead themselves? This includes colleagues, team members and direct reports.

What is the relationship between professional growth, self-leadership and discretionary effort?

As I began to say, "I only have one person to lead," did I experience a complementing release of increased energy and satisfaction? Did this energy fuel me and take me to a higher level of performance?

References

American Psychological Association. (2011, March). *Stress in the workplace*. Retrieved from:
www.apa.org/news/press/releases/phwa-survey-summary.pdf

Brandau, K. & Ross, D. (2016). *The leadership of one*. Atlanta, GA: Life Power Publishers.

Kurzweil, R. (2001, March 7). *The law of accelerating returns*. Retrieved from http://www.kurzweilai.net/the-law-of-accelerating-returns.

Rother, M. (2010). *Toyota kata: Managing people for improvement, adaptiveness, and superior results*. New York: McGraw Hill.

CHAPTER 2

Inspire Integrity at All Levels of the Organization

"Real integrity is doing the right thing, knowing that nobody's going to know whether you did it or not."
~ *Oprah Winfrey*

RossBrandau Discretionary Effort Leadership Model

PROFITABILITY AND ECONOMIC SUSTAINABILITY

Authentic Contribution

Emotional Commitment

Rational Alignment

Social Acceptance

Safety and Security

WORK ENVIRONMENT OF INTEGRITY AND GRATITUDE

Figure 2.1: Work environment of integrity and gratitude

When you become aware of the importance of a foundation of integrity and gratitude to the productivity and morale of your company, you see your deficiencies in integrity that were invisible to you before. This chapter deals with integrity and the next chapter deals with the importance of gratitude.

We begin our discussion of integrity with an experience Doug had with a manager who called a supervisor into his office and reprimanded him, "You didn't finish your quality check report."

"I know; I didn't finish it on purpose," the supervisor said.

The manager replied, "You know getting that report in on time is one of your primary responsibilities."

"Yes, but it doesn't make sense because all of the supervisors just check off all the boxes so you're not getting true data. I want you to know the reports are not being done truthfully." The manager disregarded his explanation and continued, "If you can't get your reports in on time I'll have to dock your pay. Consider this a warning."

The manager ignored the supervisor's attempt to show his integrity and surface the truth by identifying the worthlessness of reports with false data. More concerned with reports, policies and procedures than with honesty, the manager's actions destroyed trust between him and his supervisor.

Employees want to work in organizations that are known for integrity. They want to be trusted and know they can trust their managers and leaders. Organizations known for integrity are human-led value organizations that place high worth on the individual and encourage truthfulness.

> True integrity in a company is more than adherence to ethical principles.

Defining Integrity

In the course of our research, we found that integrity routinely formed the basis of company values, which makes sense. Without integrity, there is no trust. With a combination of trust and integrity, the RossBrandau Leadership Model will work. Because integrity is so fundamental to discretionary effort leadership, it is important to define what integrity means.

Integrity is a common word in the English language and one of the least understood. People seem to know what it is in their gut, but they have a hard time putting its definition into words. In the traditional way of defining integrity, dictionary.com (n.d.) identifies three distinct meanings:

1. Adherence to moral and ethical principles; soundness of moral character; honesty.
2. The state of being whole, entire, or undiminished: to preserve the integrity of the empire [organization].
3. Sound, unimpaired, or perfect condition: the integrity of a ship's hull.

All three of these definitions have applications to integrity in companies that want to live discretionary effort principles. First, individuals in companies need to adhere to ethical principles. Second, the integrity of the whole organization must be preserved. And third, the systems and procedures of the company must be sound, unimpaired, and in as perfect a condition as possible. We will address all three in this chapter. If the three elements of integrity are not met on a daily basis, the consequence is disorder, chaos, and decay represented in diminished profits and a toxic organization.

> Integrity is doing the right thing and to keep doing the next right thing until the project is complete.

In simple terms, most people define integrity as doing what they say they will do or giving your word and then keeping your word. What this definition fails to understand is that a thief has integrity when he says he will steal and he does. Since stealing is not an acceptable behavior, the definition of integrity needs to have a moral element which is about right and wrong. Integrity is about doing what is right.

The RossBrandau Leadership Model defines integrity as doing the right thing, doing the next right thing, and doing things in the right way. "Doing the right thing followed by the next right thing" is recognizing that as we work on daily tasks, decisions on future courses of action have to be made. If workers keep "do the right thing" first and foremost in their mind, bad decisions are reduced, and good decisions are increased.

Every individual from the executive suite to the maintenance supervisor and receptionist are encouraged to adhere to moral and ethical principles. Each and every person in an organization wrestles with honesty and integrity and how to define what is right. As the saying goes, one bad apple compromises the entire barrel; therefore, it is crucial for everyone to do the right thing.

A fascinating observation is that we trust ourselves to do the right thing, but question whether the person in the next office or in the cubicle across the aisle will. Often, we are not sure. This makes the development of trust a challenge because the basic instinct in people is to judge the integrity of others without being able to assess the level of their own integrity. We might question the motives of others but not our own. When decisions are not quite right, we are quick to judge others but defend our own actions.

Although we should try not to be hypocritical in evaluating ethical behaviors, this does not mean that a person of integrity is flawless and does the right thing every minute of the day. To be human is to make mistakes, errors, bad judgment calls and misconstructions. Mistakes are a fact of life and when they occur, a person of integrity is able to address the mistake, be truthful about what happened, and have an honest conversation about how to fix the problem. In an ethical environment, honesty is respected, discussions are frank and forthright, differences of opinions are expected, and conflicts are resolved through dialog.

> A person of integrity can make a mistake, correct it, and continue on the integrity journey.

The ability to have forthright conversations was a problem in one company where we consulted. When we were hired to give a workshop on difficult conversations, we found the culture of the organization was to go straight to mediation when a disagreement occurred instead of trying to resolve the conflict themselves. They were not learning to discover each other's viewpoints or the elements of negotiation. When mediation solves conflicts, someone wins and someone loses, resulting in relationships filled with resentment. Mediation is an expensive process from a budgeting standpoint, but it is costlier in relationships because people do not learn the integrity skills of taking responsibility for their actions, trusting team members, or finding solutions when they overly rely on someone else to fix the problem.

Four Qualities of Integrity

To be an influential leader, the quality of integrity is first on the list of personal character traits to be developed, nourished, and cultivated. Students of integrity define its qualities in many ways, but the four most popular are represented in Figure 2.2.

Figure 2.2: Four elements of integrity

Trust. Trust is being ethical and honest. When trust exists between individuals, they have confidence in each other and know they can rely on the other person to take responsibility for their actions and to tell the truth. Emotions of agreement and cooperation are generated.

It is also important for individuals to have future trust in each other. Future trust is a concept best explained by letting your teenager have the keys to the family car. You trust that the teenager *is* responsible and *will* bring the car back in the same condition it was in when it left the driveway. In the business world, assignments are given to individuals on the belief they will deliver so promises can be kept and integrity preserved.

Reliability. People who study personalities know one personality is characterized by a marked degree of responsibility and reliability—to a degree that almost everything else in life is subservient to fulfilling promises. A person with this personality will cross the finish line regardless of the bumps in the road.

In the workplace, a reliable employee perfectly aligns words with actions. If a supplier promises to deliver a product on a certain date, the customer receives it on that date and the quality matches the agreed upon terms. When a report is due on the manager's desk by noon, it is on the desk at noon. Before missing a deadline or delivery, a reliable person holds a candid conversation to explain why and what options are available to maintain the confidence of the recipient.

Competence. Competency is tied to reliability. It means employees have the skills stated on their resume to deliver what they promise. With that said, it is very human to accept an assignment and then freeze in fear that delivering as promised exceeds the current capability to perform. Competency demands that individuals be honest about their skill level, constantly upgrade their knowledge and abilities, and curb their ego enough to ask questions and request clarification when needed. When workers humble themselves to ask associates for help, they will find that colleagues and coworkers are usually flattered to lend their opinions and expertise.

Caring. Caring is possessing the ability to be an empathetic human being. Genuine caring for others is essential to integrity. Karla was hired by an organization to coach a non-caring manager. The manager had called an employee into her office to discuss a project deadline. Shortly into the conversation the employee broke down in tears and revealed that his wife had just been diagnosed with a fast-growing and life-threatening breast cancer. The manager looked him straight in the eye and said, "Your project is still due on Friday."

Undoubtedly there were many options this manager could have taken to show empathy for this employee and his family, but she chose not to explore any other path than to restate that the project was due. Her actions destroyed the trust not only with the employee but with the entire leadership team who disagreed with her actions. At the heart of exhibiting empathy and caring is respect for the dignity of each employee and the employee's family.

> The reality of your integrity is in the eye of the beholder.

Integrity and Leadership

When individuals in an organization adopt these four traits of integrity, mutual respect evolves with the accompanying opportunities to unwrap gifts of discretionary effort. As managers evaluate their personal four qualities of integrity, Tony Simons (2008) gives valuable insight in his book *The Integrity Dividend: Leading by the Power of Your Word*. Simons argues that leaders' personal integrity is derived by how others in the organization view them. In other words, your integrity is in the eye of the beholder. Integrity is a recognized fit between your words and your actions. Most people think they act with integrity. Even being well-intended, however, we all make mistakes based on faulty assumptions or incomplete data. This undermines our relationships with others.

Experimenting with Simons' hypothesis, Doug asked the middle managers in an organization to rate their own integrity and the integrity of their bosses on a scale of one to ten, ten being the best. They rated their own integrity on average as seven and rated their managers' integrity around eight. Next, Doug went to the front level supervisors and asked them to do the same: rate themselves and their bosses, the middle managers. This time, the front lines supervisors rated their personal integrity as seven but the middle managers lower as five or six.

Finally, the employees were asked to rate their integrity and the integrity of their front level supervisors and the middle managers. The employees rated their own integrity as seven while giving the supervisors a five and the middle managers a rating of zero or one. Not surprisingly, the middle managers dismissed the floor employee ratings as invalid and irrelevant. Simons would argue that the floor evaluations were reliable and a valid source of information on the development of personal integrity.

Since employees hear your words and see your behaviors, integrity is identified through the eye of the beholder. In fact, employees can become a valuable resource in integrity development of leaders willing to reveal a measure of honesty in their leadership skills. Individuals can believe they act with integrity, yet at times their actions may be perceived by others as being without integrity. With a certain amount of authenticity, leaders admit that their actual level of integrity in the organization stems more from others' perceptions than from their own self-perceptions. To assist in integrity development, Simons suggests evaluating these points:

- People's perception of you is a reality with which you have to deal.
- People are slow to recognize your integrity and quick to recognize your lack of it.
- People are subjective, not objective, in their judgements about your integrity.
- People seek evidence to prove their subjective perception of your integrity.
- People will discount evidence that runs counter to their perception of your integrity.
- People tend to blame you for their lack of integrity before they will blame themselves.
- People are more sensitive to your lack of integrity regarding values for which they care deeply.

While the requirement to measure integrity through the eye of the beholder may seem unfair, it is not insurmountable. Being more conscious of your integrity reputation will help you preserve your reputation and restore it when needed. A leader with integrity who operates as truthfully as possible will listen to concerns without judging and will value each person's perspective, even when the feedback means evaluating their own gaps in performance.

In one company that was working to identify the gaps in performance of the supervisors, Doug was asked to interview the most and least successful supervisors in their organization. The first manager he interviewed was called the "best in the house." Doug spent a full shift observing, walking, and talking with this best supervisor. He discovered that all of the workers on the assembly line were the supervisor's buddies. They even had television sets hidden so they could watch sports games. The environment was very collegial, and they met their targets.

The next day, Doug interviewed the worst supervisor. He was exacting and held everyone accountable. He made them arrive and leave on time. He didn't allow the crew to watch TV, and they all hated him. The employees skewed the shift's results so the supervisor wouldn't meet the performance goals that the best-in-the-house supervisor did.

Contrary to Doug's findings, the manager rewarded the supervisor who lacked work-place integrity and didn't follow the rules, but whose staff met its targets. He punished the other supervisor who tried to hold his staff accountable. The manager eventually went after this regulations-based supervisor and fired him even though he tried to supervise his employees with integrity.

Neither supervisor was relating to the employees in a way that enabled them to give discretionary effort. For the best-in-the-house supervisor, consider what results his team was capable of if everyone had spent more time producing and less time watching TV. Conversely, imagine if the rule-based supervisor would have created a more employee-friendly atmosphere. What do you think his team could have achieved with a more supportive supervisor focused on the well-being of each individual?

Organizational Integrity

"Integrity is the essence of everything successful."
~ R. Buckminster Fuller

Organizational integrity is preserved when products and services are built to specs, what was promised is delivered, and the products perform in the manner described in the sales literature. To produce products with integrity, management is responsible for project delivery systems and their constant improvement. When the workers have integrity and the systems and processes have integrity, the products and services offered by the company will be of high quality and the reputation of the company will be preserved for decades. The benefits of integrity are what led R. Buckminster Fuller (n.d.), American systems theorist, architect, engineer, and inventor of the geodesic dome, to say, "Integrity is the essence of everything successful."

Through our experience studying organizations, we can certainly affirm that integrity is a characteristic of a sustainable, profitable organization. Novartis and PricewaterhouseCoopers are two corporate examples of creating a successful organization that embodies integrity.

Integrity at Novartis

Novartis, a leading healthcare company, adopted a philosophy that places integrity at the center of their strategy for success. According to Dan Ostergaard, Head of Corporate Integrity at Novartis, "Leading companies see integrity not as an obstacle to competitiveness but as a driver of differentiation" (as cited in Novartis, n.d.).

Novartis demonstrates practical ways to implement integrity. Integrity-driven performance at Novartis means: doing the right thing, building a culture of integrity, managing risks, strengthening their reputation, and fostering a competitive advantage. Translating strategy into practice requires standards of performance for establishing, promoting, and enforcing business integrity.

For Novartis, establishing business integrity begins by translating mission and values into operational systems such as codes of conduct, policies, and management procedures. Business integrity is promoted by reflecting ethical considerations in objectives and incentives, in leadership and in training. This includes a performance assessment matrix of objectives and behaviors. Business integrity is ensured through an integrated approach to decision-making, continuous monitoring, reporting procedures, and complaints handling, as well as audits.

Integrity at PricewaterhouseCoopers

After comprehensive study, PricewaterhouseCoopers developed an integrity-driven performance standard that centers on governance, transparency, and accountability reform. Their strategy suggests that business integrity, ethics, and values do not detract from performance but add to business performance when appropriately integrated throughout the organization.

In their white paper, *Integrity Driven Performance*, PricewaterhouseCoopers (2004) introduced their performance strategy that reflects their research into the best-practices approach to governance, risk, and compliance (GRC) and adopts three core principles:

1. **Integration.** The first principle requires that organizations integrate their approach to GRC in order to foster a culture of business integrity and accountability.
2. **Coordination.** The second principle requires the effective coordination of people, processes, and technology capabilities so that an integrity-driven GRC performance strategy is embedded in the fabric of the organization.
3. **Compliance.** The third principle requires a vision of business conduct and compliance that supports compliance with both the letter and the spirit of the law. Compliance in this instance is both internal and external.

The PricewaterhouseCoopers standard for establishing a culture of integrity and ethical values suggests the GRC strategy be integrated within all the business processes along with the systems to measure compliance and effectiveness. Although PricewaterhouseCoopers and Novartis vary in the way they build upon a foundation of integrity, they both use that foundation in order to be economically sustainable.

Systems Integrity

Systems integrity encompasses the structures, procedures and processes for delivering products and services that are high quality and delivered on time. The instructions for all systems, processes, and procedures need to be easily understood and implemented. Recognizing there is always room for improvement, systems and processes need to be in the most perfect condition at any moment in time to enable the production of quality products and to ensure the safety of workers.

> For the safety of employees and the quality of your products, plan integrity into all systems, processes, and procedures.

Systems integrity is defined as freedom from as much error as is humanly possible with a continuous improvement mindset in place to keep the workplace running smoothly and profitably. The real challenge and value of systems integrity is that it is collective, not personal. It affects every aspect of the internal systems and external reputation of an organization.

Employees naturally see glitches in the processes or procedures that cause mistakes at levels leaders don't see. Some employees become angry and react openly to what they see as stupid policies or inadequate procedures in the systems. The easiest way to tap into the energy and insights of upset employees is to ask them how to fix what they see going wrong. Identifying problems and mistakes becomes the employee's opportunity to add value to the organization and to improve their personal self-worth. When leaders acknowledge their viewpoints and work with their suggestions, they form a unique bond with the employee. As the upset employees give discretionary effort to overcome the problem, they help to restore or complete the overall integrity of operations.

Ann Bernasek, in *The Economics of Integrity* (2010) argues that integrity matters--not just to our moral well-being but to our economic well-being. According to Bernasek, at the heart of the integrity of systems are four aspects:

1. **Disclosure.** Bernasek asserts that being truthful in the workplace allows employees to make their own decisions. The process of bringing issues, concerns, and problems forward is a form of disclosure that leads to a systematic solutions-oriented process where facts, assumptions and beliefs are critically examined with the goal of continuous improvement.

2. **Norms.** Furthermore, Bernasek points out that the way the majority of employees accept and follow the rules are the organizational norms. She suggests that the organization norms must reflect that the rules are clear and easy-to-follow, universally understood, and make intuitive sense. Having clarity brings efficiency and enables the system to be self-reinforcing. This, according to her, is critical in the development of systems integrity.

3. **Accountability.** The integrity of the system demands accountability. Bernasek argues that accountability is not a punishment and reward system but rather is a way to set expectations that allows natural consequences which is the basis of individual and organizational development. In every element of Mother Nature, there are natural consequences to broken rules. For instance, if you break the rule "Don't step off the second level platform," then the natural consequence is you are subject to the law of gravity. Similarly, in organizations, if rules are broken, there are consequences.

4. **Continuous improvement.** Integrity, in the behaviors of both management and security systems, demands continuous improvement in the

> commitment to drive out overburdening,
> unreasonable, or absurd elements of the system.
> Continuous improvement keeps the integrity of the
> systems intact.

The integrity goal is for management to acknowledge risks and hazards, take responsibility, and be directly accountable for the reliability of the security and safety systems. Then, when all the requisite systems are in place and predictably executed, workers will trust their leaders and the organization, and they will feel safe. With that trust, employees can mentally and emotionally move toward giving the discretionary effort that moves the organization forward.

Products and services that meet and then exceed their guarantees lead to profitability. To produce products with integrity, management is responsible for the predictability of the project delivery systems and their constant improvement. Some, who think nothing of offering inferior products or services to the marketplace, may think integrity and trust are not profitable traits.

The correlation between the degree of integrity and performance in the marketplace is not a secret, but a well-understood phenomenon. The ultimate goal for an organization is to design and build products, services, and structures with integrity so the marketplace will trust the organization and its products. Every organization enjoys the rewards of its integrity by attracting and retaining loyal customers. As the company delivers increasingly higher quality products and services, the company evolves, progresses, and prosperity ensues.

Rebuilding Trust

In today's world, we face the reality that the employer-employee relationship is much more complex than it was in the early 20th century work-for-wages and benefits pattern. The question becomes: how can leaders rebuild trust that was lost during an economic downturn or in changes of promised policies and procedures, such as post-retirement benefits? How can they rebuild trust and retain their intelligent and capable workers?

Further, 21st century employers can no longer afford to remain competitive merely by providing the traditional pension plans and health care benefits of days gone by. The projections for life expectancy, advances in medical technology, and the spiking cost trends of health care and prescription drugs have made those promises unsustainable. Even if employees know the reality of this situation, they probably won't welcome any changes to their benefits package. Therefore, with the inevitable decision to modify pension plans and eliminate post-retirement health care, the employees' loyalty to the company dissipates. Loyalty will continue to exist, but it will shift to a leader or a work group, making interpersonal relationships and the attention to workplace well-being critical.

The Practice of Discretionary Effort

Leadership of One Power Principle: Be the leader people choose to follow by doing the right thing, doing the next right thing, and doing things the right way.

Reflection

Integrity involves doing the right thing, then doing the next right thing, and doing things the right way. This philosophy should apply to individuals, organizations, and systems. A leader of integrity ensures there is a recognizable fit between words and actions. When leaders do the right things, there is an ordered relationship between actions and results that people can rely on. This releases discretionary effort with an accompanying increase in performance and results.

·When there is integrity in individuals, the discretionary effort employees offer their leaders creates money through increased productivity and problem-solving activities. Integrity in organizational systems is likewise critical to profits because ultimately, economic success depends on supplying customers with a good product that matches or exceeds the sales pitch. Good products lead to increased sales and not the other way around.

Discretionary Effort Exercise:

Do the Right Thing, Do the Next Right Thing, and Do Things the Right Way

The practice of doing the right thing begins with simple things like ensuring that you do nothing careless to hurt anyone physically. It requires that you pay attention when you are doing everyday actions, like cutting the grass or driving the car. It then progresses to making decisions at work that ensure you meet customer needs in an orderly way. You know you are doing the right thing when there are no reworks and your customers' needs are met.

When you are doing the next right thing, you are operating with integrity (your actions and words are consistent and support each other). Through integrity, work and life unfold in an orderly pattern with predictable results. When you are operating with duplicity (your actions and words are inconsistent and do not support each other), work and life unfold in a disorderly manner with unintended consequences that you or someone has to remedy.

The exercise for this chapter is to practice doing the right thing, doing the next right thing, and doing things the right way. A signal of integrity is a feeling of completeness and satisfaction. When you do the wrong thing, correct it. When you run into unintended consequences, do the right thing. When you think you have done the right thing, do the next right thing at home, at work, and with everyone you encounter.

Daily practice of doing the right thing, doing the next right thing, and doing things the right way develops integrity within you. Others will want to stay within your influence of integrity and to develop integrity within themselves.

Discretionary Effort Practice Steps

Step 1: Observe and Experience. In the course of your day, be mindful of doing the right thing, doing the next right thing, and doing things the right way. Look for feeling of completeness that validates your choice.

Step 2: Contemplate and Record. Maintain a record of your experiences of doing right as part of your understanding of developing individual integrity.

Step 3: Share, Learn and Model. After you have evaluated the following questions, share your insights and ask for input from a mentor, a friend, or trusted advisor.

1. What were my breakthroughs about my personal integrity? Did I experience any breakdowns in personal integrity? What was the impact of the breakthrough or the breakdown in my life?
2. What breakthroughs or breakdowns did I observe in the integrity of other individuals, the organization, or organizational systems?
3. What is the relationship between doing the right thing and discretionary effort?
4. How can I model integrity in all of my actions and words?

References

Bernasek, A. (2010). *The economics of integrity.* New York: HarperCollins Publishers

Fuller, R. B. (n.d.). *BrainyQuote.com.* Retrieved from http://www.brainyquote.com/quotes/authors/r/r_buckminster_fuller.html

Integrity. (n.d.). In *Dictionary.com Unabridged*. Retrieved from http://www.dictieary.com/browse/integrity

Novartis (n.d.). *Integrity and compliance at Novartis*. Retrieved from https://www.scribd.com/document/51904323/Integrity-and-compliance

PricewaterhouseCoopers (2004). *Integrity driven performance*. Retrieved from http://www.grc-resource.com/resources/pwc_integritydrivenperformance.pdf

Simons, T. (2008). *The integrity dividend: Leading by the power of your word*. San Francisco: Jossey-Bass.

CHAPTER 3

The Power of Gratitude

"It's not happy people who are thankful.
It's thankful people who are happy."
~ Anonymous

The second foundational principle running parallel to integrity in the RossBrandau Leadership Model is the power of gratitude. Gratitude is a foreign notion in many organizations but the concept has attracted scholarly researchers, including Dr. Robert Emmons, a professor at the University of California, Davis. As one of the leading scholars in the scientific study of gratitude, he said the following in his book *Thanks! How the New Science of Gratitude Can Make You Happier*:

> "It is possible that psychology has ignored gratitude because it appears, on the surface, to be a very obvious emotion, lacking in interesting complications: we receive a gift—from friends, from family, from God—and then we feel pleasurably grateful. But while the emotion seemed simplistic even to me, as I began my research, I soon discovered that gratitude is a deeper, more complex phenomenon that plays a critical role in human happiness. Gratitude is literally one of the few things that can measurably change people's lives." (2007)

Through scientific study, Dr. Emmons and other researchers have documented what the title of the book states: grateful people are happy. Said in a little different way, David Steindl-Rast, a Benedictine monk penned these words: "It is not joy that makes us grateful; it is gratitude that makes us joyful." Morale and discretionary effort are increased if the company culture makes gratitude an essential part of human interactions and managers express appreciation and thanks on a regular basis.

> Giving more than is required, anticipated or expected is giving discretionary effort.

To put the power of gratitude to work in your company, managers need not do anything exceptional; they just need to be grateful for the efforts of their employees. In the course of every day work, opportunities arise that if acted on by employees will take the organization to the next level. When the actions are acknowledged and gratitude is expressed, people pay attention and are rejuvenated in a mysterious way. Giving discretionary effort provides a new way of contributing to the organization.

Leaders in this incredibly complex and challenging world are constantly looking for ideas to motivate, empower, and inspire the people in their organizations to new heights. They implicitly know that people are their essential value creation instrument and that each and every person has the capability and capacity to make a difference in the organization. People are at the heart of every exchange, whether it is between external customers and the organization or just between team members.

What individuals do in any situation, in each exchange, is a matter of choice. They can do the minimum, what is expected, or they can choose to do more than what is expected. When they do more than is expected, they choose to give discretionary effort.

Creating a culture in a company where discretionary effort is freely given by employees is connected to acknowledging and expressing gratitude for each employee's hard work. Building a culture of gratitude does not involve learning new competencies, improving strategic planning, or changing performance metrics. It does not mean sacrificing leadership responsibility or accountabilities.

What it does mean is that you build a culture of gratitude where discretionary effort is acknowledged on a regular, in-the-moment basis. In simple terms, a culture of gratitude means you live by the golden rule: Treat others as you would like to be treated. We learned this rule as kids in kindergarten. Recognizing discretionary effort with a simple thank you doesn't cost a dime yet has huge monetary payoffs.

Gratitude as a Genius Strategy

Acts of discretionary effort are easy to be taken for granted, but once a culture of gratitude is established, it becomes a genius strategy for company growth. The Oxford Dictionary defines genius as an "exceptional intellectual or creative power or other natural ability." The second definition is one we don't expect: "the prevailing character or spirit of something." This is the goal—to make a culture of gratitude the prevailing spirit of the company.

As mentioned, genius can be a natural ability, a creative power or an exceptional contribution. We all have seen genius manifested in individuals such as Nelson Mandela, Albert Einstein, Marie Curie, Nicola Tesla, Maya Angelo, or Stephen Hawking to name a few. Each of these men and women made exceptional contributions to their field of expertise.

Not every employee has the potential to be a Stephen Hawking, but what would happen if we looked at all employees as having the natural ability and creative power to make a significant contribution with their genius within their sphere of control? What would happen if we stopped looking for genius outside of the company and start cultivating the genius inside the company? Our experience has taught us that if you start acknowledging people as having the natural ability to contribute in significant ways, people will step up to meet the expectations and fulfill the definition of genius.

> Expressing gratitude for workers' discretionary effort is the key to increased productivity.

As an example, an elderly school janitor, who spoke very little English, was talking to his manager about excessive amounts of paper in storage. He lamented the high cost of inventory and the wasted space required to store it in a specific climate-controlled environment. He inquired gently if he could ask the suppliers to deliver a certain predetermined amount each month. It was a genius suggestion.

Doug's five-year-old boy was having a discussion one day with him, and he showed pure genius for such a little guy. He said, "People like to fix things, don't they?" Doug replied, "You're right." The boy was silent for a moment and then stated, "They think the world is broken, don't they." He quietly replied again, "You're probably right." After another period of silence, he stated, "Well, they are wrong. The world is not broken."

Doug sighed and realized that he and many others were busy trying to fix the world by fixing their broken companies. What if everyone on earth just sat back and saw the world and their company as fine, not perfect, but perfectly wonderful? With this viewpoint, they would experience less stress and enjoy their personal and professional lives more on a daily basis.

Who would have thought an elderly janitor could identify and offer solutions to a problem that was costing hundreds of thousands of dollars of waste throughout the entire school system? Who could conceive that a five-year-old boy could assess the world and pronounce an entirely positive point of view that could impact the lives of millions of people?

People have a natural ability to contribute value-added solutions. Instead of installing suggestion boxes and establishing reward programs, take the time to help your workers become geniuses in their sphere of influence and cultivate a culture that implements their genius suggestions.

Character Gifts and Genius

Everyone has a genius aptitude or innate talent that contributes to the overall success of the company. These talents and aptitudes are the hidden gifts leaders should look for as they seek to earn the discretionary effort of employees.

To discover these genius gifts, look deeper at the plethora of talents each individual has that may not be precisely work-related but contributes to the total skills everyone brings to the company. One employee was a shooting range instructor on weekends. He had a keen sense of accuracy. Recognizing this talent, his manager arranged for him to work on quality control processes, putting his skills to work on precision equipment calibration.

Taking a closer look at the talents of employees helps you observe employees listening carefully to each other, exhibiting compassion and empathy for those going through tough times, demonstrating business acumen when looking for marketplace solutions, and mediating disagreements. Some employees excel in computer interests such as networking, programming, creating documents and so forth. Other gifts and talents include an uncanny ability to read social conversations and determine what to do and say. Some people have a gift of seeing how space and ergonomics should work in the office building. Having a rational perspective and being adept at looking at a situation from an objective viewpoint is another gift.

Gratitude and Surfacing the Truth

Another gift is to be authentic and to speak truthfully when dealing with misunderstandings and conflict. Truth is the state of being real or actual. In 21st century organizations, surfacing the truth is one of the most significant strategies for resolving systemic problems yet many leaders are not grateful for this gift of truth.

> Expressing gratitude gives employees the courage to share a wide range of character gifts with the company.

One of Doug's clients took over a major manufacturing organization. Doug's client quickly learned that the previous leader had manipulated the results to put the organization in a better light with its stockholders. The client lamented to Doug about how difficult it was to fix the real problems when people were used to dealing with the misrepresentations of reality, where the truth was never surfaced.

At another plant, Doug listened to a manager brag about incredible quality results for his organization. Doug asked him how he measured quality. The manager replied, "Our measurement of quality is based on our clients' feedback, and their feedback is great."

Doug asked, "Do you ever measure product quality at the source, before it goes to the customer?"

"No, that's not necessary," he replied, "We're already breaking all the quality records in the industry." This manager was all about *looking* good. He did not realize that measuring quality at the source was about *being* good.

Leaders need to know the reality of every situation. Reality is often not what they think it is or what they want it to be. Often employees have a better picture of reality than the leadership team but they don't surface the truth because they don't want to disturb their boss's version of reality with the facts. They know the boss won't be grateful for them uncovering the truth and they may face retribution.

Being open to and grateful for the opinions of each individual is a genius strategy for every leader. At the minimum, it is an opportunity to inform, educate, and inspire the employees to see a different perspective, the leader's perspective. At the maximum, every employee is capable of identifying and pointing out the truth about situations that may otherwise eventually sink the company. Be grateful for those employees who are brave enough to surface the truth.

> It takes a mature manager to be grateful for employees surfacing the truth as they see and experience it.

Transforming a Negative Environment

Human nature chooses negativity more frequently than positivity. Knowing this, it is understandable why most individuals focus on problems, disturbances, annoyances, barriers and injustices—the negatives—rather than the positive things that happen each day for which they can be grateful. This preoccupation with negativity is not healthy, and when the leader focuses on negativity, the workers will do the same.

We are not advocating behaviors that conceal problems or having an unrealistic "ignorance is bliss" attitude. In order to establish a culture of gratitude, we simply ask that leaders look on the positive side of life and be thankful for what is given to them as individuals. Then through the lens of gratitude, leaders look for and acknowledge the silent, unnoticed gifts employees quietly give. This will have a powerful, positive effect on the daily work environment.

A 2009 study published in the *Journal of Personality* showed that adults who feel grateful are more optimistic, report more social satisfaction, experience less envy, less depression, and fewer physical complaints. They also sleep better and get more exercise. Kids who experience more gratitude do better in school, set higher goals for themselves, derive more satisfaction from life, friends, and family, are generally less materialistic, and have more desire to give back (Kashdan, Mishra, Breen & Froh, 2009).

Gratitude also has a social benefit. Referring again to gratitude research by Robert Emmons (2007), people who are assigned the task of making a daily gratitude list are more likely to report having helped someone with a personal problem or having offered emotional support to another. On the other hand, those who do not express daily gratitude are more likely to focus on the hassles of life or negatively compare themselves to others. Little does it matter what you are experiencing in life, for gratitude has the power to change your perspective to focus on the positive rather than the negative.

It is important that gratitude lives in the present tense, meaning that when you see people doing something extra, thank them immediately. When undertaken daily in a conscious and mindful manner, the expression of gratitude to employees for their discretionary efforts changes the culture of the organization. Employees begin to look at the future, not with rose colored glasses, but with realistic hopes for achievement and success.

The Multiplier Effect of Gratitude

Cultivating genius, surfacing the truth, and turning negativity to gratitude paves the way for incredible exponential growth opportunities in any organization. The website *businessdictionary.com* defines exponential growth as the "Increase in number or size, at a constantly growing rate. It is one possible result of a reinforcing feedback loop that makes a population or system grow (escalate) by increasingly higher volumes." Gratitude has a multiplier effect on productivity and discretionary effort.

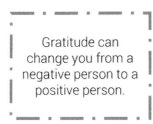

Gratitude can change you from a negative person to a positive person.

The gift of discretionary effort is released in the organization one act at a time. Using the concept of exponential growth, we can set out this hypothetical scenario: One manager chooses to practice gratitude by acknowledging the discretionary efforts of one employee, one situation at a time. On day one, the manager takes the time to recognize one person in one situation. On day two, she not only notices the same person releasing more discretionary effort by giving a practice improvement suggestion, but she also sees another employee contributing a little more than expected by helping another employee with a spreadsheet.

In theory, the second employee observed the first employee giving discretionary effort and witnessed the gratitude expressed. This second employee follows the first employee's example to earn a similar expression of gratitude. We now have twice as much discretionary effort released into the organization compared to the starting point.

The whole idea of exponentials or compound interest is that with gratitude, discretionary effort grows exponentially. Two incidents become four incidents, which become eight incidents, which become sixteen incidents, and so on.

When a leader acknowledges discretionary effort with gratitude, employees feel good and naturally want to start the cycle over by giving more, receiving thanks, and feeling good again. Others, witnessing the gratitude that was expressed, want the same recognition for themselves and without knowing why, they imitate what they have seen. At some point, discretionary effort and acknowledgement multiply to the level where employees are contributing in the most clever and powerful ways they can. Contributions by employees, whether it's through their innate talents and skills or their gifts of discretionary effort, are an important ingredient in value creation, profitability and economic sustainability for the company.

> Once a culture of gratitude is started in a company, it has a multiplier effect like a snowball rolling downhill.

Gratitude works because it is a fundamental principle of living and it has been proven time and time again as an important part of building community and team work in organizations. It matters not the size, importance, or shape of the contribution—all contributions are important in different ways. When leaders take on the practice of being grateful for the discretionary effort they observe, the efforts of team members to be polite and to say thank you to each other is enhanced.

Within a culture of gratitude, a team member might guilelessly advise someone on a resolution to an issue on a project without even being aware he or she gave anything. A young enthusiastic employee could suddenly and unexpectedly provide a solution to a problem he or she did not even know existed as they are mentored by a seasoned team member. There are many little ways gratitude makes a big impact on the workplace culture.

The Leader's Gratitude Challenge

The opportunity for changing the work environment from negativity to a culture of gratitude is monumental for the leadership team, a manager or a team leader. The journey starts with the simple step of looking around the office and observing what employees are doing for each other.

Who stayed late to help the team finish the project due tomorrow morning at 8:00 a.m.? Who covered for Olivia when she had a dentist appointment? Who volunteered to help Evan in accounting when he was buried with end of the year close-outs? Who made time in their schedule to plan the holiday party? Observe these actions and tell the individuals thank you. An unbelievable chain of events will start. Like a smile that doubles when you give it away, being grateful for observable kindnesses at work will double the efforts of all employees.

The leader's gratitude challenge that will change the culture of the organization involves simple actions. One strategy is to consciously change the way you see the world outside of your cubicle or office from "nothing is ever right" to "I'm grateful for _____ (name what *is* working)." As you do, you will change your little corner of the world. The power is within every individual to make the environment and the team a happier place on a daily basis.

Another approach is to find at least one person every day you can recognize for his or her gifts of kindness, thoughtfulness, and discretionary effort. Sincerely say thank you. Only one thank you message a day will suffice. Express gratitude in person, in a well-worded email, or a hand-written note.

> Your challenge:
> Notice an act of discretionary effort and thank the employee on a daily basis.

Karla once asked a colleague who had just joined her company if he could ever remember being thanked for a job well done. There was a long pause; in fact, there was complete silence for at least a minute while he sorted through all the files in his brain. He said, "No, I cannot remember in my entire career when a manager looked me in the eye and said thank you for the extra effort you gave on your project." He had won several sales awards, but those were trophies given at the annual banquet.

He remembered when the owners of the small company he worked for had given him time off and tickets to go watch his daughter play her last college basketball game at Duke University. This was indeed a gesture of appreciation, but he could not remember a single time a manager had shaken his hand and said the words, "Thank you" to his face.

Simple words of appreciation are easily lost in the corporate world. In our do-more-with-less world, some organizations inadvertently implement a mindset that tries to extract every last bit of energy out of their workers on a daily basis. These environments lack the energy, innovation, and ingenuity that gratitude creates.

An important mindset change is to think of employees as having more to give—a lot more to give—if their leaders established the right environment to do so. As an example, a quiet frontline supervisor came up with a radical idea to help the production line of a manufacturing company achieve its targets. His idea was simple and inexpensive.

The suggestion provoked a lot of interest with the management team and led to many weeks of discussions involving corporate accountants, lawyers, consultants, and so on. In the end, the frontline supervisor's proposed idea was totally revamped by the management team. The simple idea to save money was replaced with a concept completely different and five times more expensive with a much longer project time line.

The president sat down with this fellow and informed him they were not going with his solution. The supervisor begged for one last opportunity to explain the plan. He took the president out on the floor and explained the concept. It was so simple. The president asked the supervisor what he needed and how much time the implementation would take. He replied he needed five men over the weekend and a budget that was five times less than the one allocated for the managers' overhaul of the original approach. There would be no downtime. The president said yes.

Two weekends later, a team led by the supervisor went to work. They gave discretionary effort, and the new system was in place the next Monday morning. Within two weeks, production had significantly increased.

This scenario illustrates what can happen when employees are given the chance to shine. It is the responsibility of the leadership team to create the environment in their organization where employees can open their gifts, be recognized and thanked, and have the opportunity to give more.

Giving and Receiving Gifts of Discretionary Effort

Why does a culture of gratitude increase productivity? It comes down to human emotions. We feel good inside of ourselves when we contribute in worthwhile ways. If we are acknowledged for our contributions, we feel important. Feeling important, we are inspired to add more value in the world around us, and this creates an upward spiral of constantly increasing effort, energy, and productivity.

Deep inside, most employees want to give more because their self-esteem and self-worth is enhanced when they produce value-added work. If they are burned out from too many requests to produce more in less time and are not acknowledged, they may lose hope that their gifts of answering the urgent call to action and giving of discretionary effort will ever be recognized.

Not recognizing their unselfish acts of giving of time and energy is a refusal to accept their gift of discretionary effort. If leaders do not recognize the employee gifts that go beyond just fulfilling their job description, it is as though the employee never contributed. Their giving wanes, and in time may cease, leaving a hollowness inside the company.

> Noticing and mentioning the gifts of discretionary effort enhances the employee's feeling of self-esteem and builds emotional commitment to the leader and the company.

In contrast, when a leader accepts and is grateful for the gift of discretionary effort the employee gives, the acknowledgement enhances the employees' feeling of self-worth. Their emotional commitment to the leader and to the organization increases.

In reality, the giving and the receiving doesn't happen only between a manager and an employee. The giving and receiving frequently happens between two team members. As the giving and receiving occurs, both the giver and the receiver are enhanced and team relationships are strengthened.

The giver has the intent of making the receiver feel welcomed, wanted, and worthy. When the receiver gratefully accepts the gift of discretionary effort, the giver also feels welcomed, wanted, and worthy. Superior, trusting relationships evolve, and superior, trusting relationships make the wheels of business turn.

As these interactions occur, the culture of gratitude is established. The final step in the leadership challenge is to see the gifts that are being given around you and be grateful for them. When actively looking for small actions from others in the company that you can be grateful for, you will start to see contributions on an hourly basis. Your task is to acknowledge them, accept them, and express thanks. As you display an attitude of gratitude, discretionary effort will increase among your employees.

The Practice of Discretionary Effort

LEADERSHIP OF ONE POWERFUL PRINCIPLE

Leadership of One Power Principle: Be the leader people choose to follow by developing an aptitude for noticing and expressing gratitude.

Reflection

Establishing an aptitude for noticing and expressing gratitude is a genius strategy because it releases the natural talents and character gifts of every employee. Being grateful for the contribution of each worker creates an environment where individuals can surface the truth. They are allowed to see problems, suggest solutions, and work to fix nagging, everyday problems.

As an attitude of gratitude spreads in an organization, negativity can turn into optimism and hope for a bright future. Gratitude is a fundamental life principle and an essential component in creating a human-led value organization that recognizes human dignity. Thanking every worker for unselfish actions in completing tasks increases their feelings of self-worth and increases morale.

Discretionary Effort Exercise:

I Have Everything I Need

The next time you face a major challenge, take a moment and rationally think about everything you have at your disposal that could solve the problem. Taking a moment for reflection can provide a great sense of self-reliance and gratitude.

The human tendency is to focus on what you don't have (the negative perspective) in contrast to being grateful for what you do have (the positive perspective). On a company level, some rationalize that the reason they are not successful in the marketplace is because of the things they don't have—enough staff, time, money, etc.

You take a stand for success as you appreciate the gifts, talents, and treasures you see in your employees and rationally believe that while you may not have everything you would ideally like, you have everything you need to get the job done. You recognize a multitude of resources the organization has, see the potential, and make the organization more self-reliant, sustainable, and profitable.

There are many possible types of employee talents, skills, and gifts you have at your disposal: experience, knowledge, foresight, planning, determination, and collaboration to name a few. The question becomes how to place the talents and gifts of employees in the right places to give you and the organization everything you need to succeed in the marketplace.

The practice for this chapter is to think "I am grateful we have everything we need to succeed" as you attend meetings and enter into discussions to resolve pressing organizational issues. Recognizing that you have everything you need develops the aptitude for gratitude. Saying this repeatedly allows you to create the extra energy and mental clarity within you needed to overcome major challenges. As your determination and optimism to succeed spreads to everyone you touch, the giving of discretionary effort will increase.

Discretionary Effort Practice Steps

Step 1: Observe and Experience. In the course of your day, be grateful for everything you have at your fingertips to produce what you need to succeed in reaching your goals. Be grateful for the gifts of discretionary effort you observe. When you are infected with the scarcity mentality, ask yourself: What is really needed in this circumstance? What resources are already in place that can help us reach our goal? What is the right thing to do?

Step 2: Contemplate and Record. Maintain a record of your experiences of being grateful for everything you have to produce what you need at this moment in time. You may need more in the future, but focus on the present.

Step 3: Share, Learn, and Model. After you have evaluated the following questions, share your insights and ask for input from a mentor, a friend, or trusted advisor.

1. What personal breakthroughs did I gain by being grateful for what I have? Did I experience a breakdown when I did not have everything at my fingertips that can solve the challenges confronting me?
2. What breakdowns occurred as result of people thinking they didn't have everything they needed and were working from fear, not gratitude?
3. What is the relationship between gratitude and discretionary effort?
4. How can I model recognizing that I have everything I need so others adopt the same approach?

References

Emmons, R. A. (2007). *Thanks!: How the new science of gratitude can make you happier*. Boston: Houghton Mifflin Company.

Exponential growth. (n.d.). In *BusinessDictionary.com*. Retrieved from http://www.businessdictionary.com/definition/exponential-growth.html

Genius. (n.d.). In Oxford dictionaries online. *Oxford University Press*. Retrieved from

http://www.oxforddictionaries.com/us/definition/
american_english/genius

Kashdan, T. B., Mishra, A., Breen, W. E., & Froh, J. J. (2009). Gender differences in gratitude: Examining appraisals, narratives, the willingness to express emotions, and changes in psychological needs. *Journal of Personality*, 77(3), 691-730.

Steindl-Rast, D. (1984). *Gratefulness, the Heart of Prayer: An Approach to Life in Fullness.* Ramsey, NJ: Paulist Press.

CHAPTER 4

Leadership Level 1:
Safety and Security

"After the Challenger accident, NASA put in a lot of time to improve the safety of the space shuttle to fix the things that had one wrong."
~ *Sally Ride, American Physicist and Astronaut*

RossBrandau Discretionary Effort Leadership Model

PROFITABILITY AND ECONOMIC SUSTAINABILITY

Authentic Contribution

Emotional Commitment

Rational Alignment

Social Acceptance

Safety and Security

WORK ENVIRONMENT OF INTEGRITY AND GRATITUDE

Figure 4.1: Leadership Level 1, Safety and Security

Providing employees with a work environment where they feel safe from external and internal threats is the first level in the

RossBrandau Leadership Model. As shown in Figure 4.1, safety and security are essential to the other leadership levels.

Safety is the way organizations define, implement, and prevent **internal** threats such as accidents, the spread of communicable diseases, slips and falls, back injuries, etc. in the workplace. It comes from the Latin word *salvus* which means healthy.

Security refers to the way organizations detect, prevent, and respond to **external** threats such as theft, sabotage, and terrorism. It comes from the Latin word *secure* which means free of concern. Accordingly, a workplace that is security- and safety-conscious is designed to create a healthy environment free of concern.

When employees feel safe, they are free to give discretionary effort and concentrate their energies on innovating, cost cutting, customer service, solving problems, and improving processes—not protecting themselves from bodily harm or injury. Thus, the return on investment for safety and well-being initiatives is increased profitability.

If safety and security concerns are not in place in the organization, employees spend most of their energy looking over their shoulder so they are not blindsided by dangerous situations. This allocation of energy is nonproductive to the overarching organizational purposes and distracts the employees from completing their tasks. Lack of personal security and safety creates an environment of *ill-being* where people are uneasy and inhibited as they perform normal activities required by their job description. Well-being, not ill-being, is the 21st century goal.

The focus of 20th century leadership was on a healthy and safe internal workplace. Today many companies and organizations pride themselves in well-developed health and safety systems that meet and exceed government regulations. This is a significant accomplishment and employees feel that company leaders and the government have their best interest when it comes to health and safety.

Leadership in the 21st century will improve 20th century internal safety systems by developing external security systems. An easy way to think of it is that safety is creating an accident-free environment while security is creating an anxiety-free environment. Safety involves averting the threats that are known through decades of observation and practice. Security is working to anticipate and minimize the effects of unknown threats that intrude into the workplace.

> Lack of personal security and safety creates an environment of ill-being, not well-being.

Increasingly, we see a variety of threats from external attacks. In today's social media environment, people are concerned about identity theft, credit card violations, physical attacks and online defamation of character. At the company level worldwide, there is a rise in workplace violence and an increase in organizational espionage. Recent acts of terrorism expose the vulnerabilities of organizations and the high price paid for inadequate security measures.

When systems are in place ensuring internal safety and external security, employees have confidence they will walk out of the workplace at night in the same shape they walked in that morning.

Workplace Safety Adds Value to Your Business

Since the inception of factories at the beginning of the 20th century, workplace safety, especially the prevention of accidents, has been a critical issue for manufacturing firms. As work transitioned to an office environment, safety concerns stayed top of mind in all organizations for understandable monetary reasons: reduced medical costs, attorney fees, worker's compensation, time away from work, and hiring new individuals due to turnover.

Workplace safety is any interaction between the human body and the physical environment. Safety is concerned with the prevention of accidents, the spread of communicable diseases, eliminating slips and falls, and eradicating carpel tunnel. According to the United States Department of Labor (n.d.), "Businesses spend $170 billion a year on costs associated with occupational injuries and illnesses nationwide – expenditures that come straight out of company profits." Likewise, studies show that the $170 billion for the expenses of injuries at work is the equivalent to the annual costs of cancer (Leigh, Markowitz, Fahs & Landrigan, 2000).

To anyone looking from the outside in, these appear to be superficial and selfish corporate reasons. But looking from the inside out, leaders recognize that people are their greatest investment. The more invested, the greater the return. Safe workplaces are healthy workplaces, and they yield more satisfied, creative workers, better customer service and higher quality products.

> Actively promoting workplace safety and the minimizing of accidents promotes a healthy bottom-line.

Many workplace accidents and hazards are totally preventable if proper precautions are taken. It is important to require compliance to all rules and regulations by each employee and that the company provides preventive safety measures, training and equipment to:

- Reduce workplace accidents of all kinds
- Eliminate repetitive motion injuries
- Avoid back and neck injuries
- Remove asbestos and lead dangers
- Improve air quality and HVAC comfort
- Eliminate environmental hazards
- Prevent communicable diseases
- Maintain clean and sanitary conditions throughout the building

Continuous improvement of the systems and processes that ensure safety need to be regularly evaluated. These evaluations should include:

- All safety programs and policies that are operating in the company

- Processes, procedures, and practices that ensure best health practices
- Goals and objectives that drive continuous improvement of safety systems
- Inspections to identify potential workplace hazards
- Program audits to ensure personal and organizational responsibilities are being met
- Hazard identification and control to prevent accidents

Tracking and measuring success with metrics improves safety programs. Various management gurus throughout the decades have advocated measurement. Management consultant and author Peter Drucker very succinctly said, "What's measured improves" (goodreads.com, n.d.). Karl Pearson is credited with establishing the

> Workplace safety minimizes threats in the actual work environment. Security neutralizes threats from outside the company.

discipline of mathematical statistics and coining Pearson's Law which reads: "That which is measured improves. That which is measured and reported improves exponentially" (Positioning Systems Blog, 2008). Taking this statement to heart, it is essential your company not only evaluates safety and security programs but includes measurements to document progress so that performance can truly improve.

Two other essential elements in the safety mix are employee involvement and communication. To get employees involved, form committees to promote safety education. Maintain awareness through a variety of communication methods. Convey safety messages through memos, emails, and posters. Remind your managers to emphasize safety in their personal conversations with employees.

True safety in a company is a concerted effort by many forces. Through increased attention and focus, governments, companies, and individuals have worked together to develop integrated systems for safety that are continually improving. As safety consciousness has been elevated, workers are more aware of the consequences of poor safety attitudes and behaviors. Governments have increased penalties for non-conformance and companies regularly assess workman compensation costs as a bottom-line financial performance indicator.

Evolving Workplace Security Measures

Working in tandem with safety is workplace security. As we turn to security, it is a present and a future challenge, meaning that no one can predict what security challenges will arise as we progress through the 21st century. In the same way safety measures developed in the 20th century, 21st century security systems will become more sophisticated as organizations increase their attention to protecting the company, their products and their employees. Security will evolve in a similar manner as safety.

Today, lighting around buildings is a critical factor in security and is taken for granted. When it is missing, people are nervous and afraid of what might be lurking in the dark. Other security strategies are designed to deal with everything from fire and theft to bomb scares and personal emergency procedures. Companies are responsible to provide security, not just for the employees walking from the building to their cars after dark, but also for their cars parked in the parking lot. Proper lighting, reduced trees and shrubs, cameras and alarm systems are technological solutions for security.

Companies also opt to hire security guards who physically protect workers from vagrants, thieves, and any individual with a perceived intent of criminal activities from entering the building. Guards prevent theft or vandalism of company equipment and supplies while deterring illegal or inappropriate actions. They do this by maintaining high visibility, wearing uniforms to represent their lawful authority, observing those coming and going, physically, via video cameras and taking actions that minimize dangerous situations.

It may not be practical for your company to hire a security guard or put in metal detectors and X-ray machines, but all organizations can take preventative measures by evaluating their policies and procedures, such as:

- Emergency response systems
- Workplace violence deterrence
- Data security and cyber-attack prevention programs
- Fire protection systems
- Emergency response systems
- Bomb threat evacuation training

A fundamental truth is that security attacks will always occur at the weakest link. Accordingly, companies will work to counteract and strengthen their weakest link. Finding the weakest link becomes a continuous improvement strategy as when one weak link is corrected, the next flaw becomes evident. Continually improving and going forward, confronting and grappling with threats makes workplace security an evolving process.

In the end, if the company is able to overcome their vulnerabilities, then security puts the company ahead of the competition based on the number of employees who choose to stay with the company knowing they are physically safe on the premises.

Two Sides of the Same Coin

Safety and security are two sides of the same coin. If organizations are not continually updating their strategies for safety and not introducing new security systems, outdated methods quickly become a deficiency. Employees are a significant source of discovering defects. Management teams intent on 21st century safety and security will listen carefully to employees' observations and concerns without equating these concerns with complaints. If workers are labeled as complainers and troublemakers by giving sincere observations, they may become fearful, alienated and disengaged. By their silence, real hazards could be overlooked.

If given permission, most employees will take the opportunity to point out potential dangers. When they speak up, they are giving discretionary effort. As previously stated, employees feel valued when management listens to them. This is a significant factor in bringing order to a process that might be on the verge of chaos in an environment that may have inadvertently changed overnight.

Here are three ways you can put employees at the center of safety and security in the organization:

- Recognize that employees see and encounter security and safety challenges every day.
- Listen to what employees say about necessary changes to each policy and procedure.
- Make employees responsible and accountable for recognizing and reporting security and safety issues to both their coworkers and management.

The State of Well-Being

As Doug consulted in organizations, he discovered that attention to safety and security results in a sense of well-being among employees. Well-being is a general term indicating the condition of an individual's existence. Normally, a high sense of well-being describes a positive state of health, happiness, and prosperity. A low sense of well-being indicates a negative state of chronic health conditions, undesirable emotions, and possibly a lack of sufficient income. Doug noticed that including a focus on the whole person by providing in-house fitness facilities, a staff trainer and a cafeteria offering a healthy choice of foods was an enhancement to well-being and company morale.

> Companies that actively pursue well-being for each employee have a more productive workforce.

In relationship to discretionary effort, we will discuss three areas that indicate well-being: social, emotional and psychological. The higher the social, emotional and psychological well-being indicators, individual well-being rises. When individual well-being is high, the potential for discretionary effort increases.

Karla learned about individual well-being in the social, emotional, and psychological realm in a retail store. As she stood in line to check out, the woman in front of her was attempting to return an item she had purchased from the neighboring county with a higher sales tax. The woman was insisting that the store refund the seven extra cents of sales tax collected from the other county. The sales associate was kind and empathetic as she explained that she was not allowed to do that as per company policy. The woman became irate. This little dispute over seven cents was holding up nearly ten customers waiting to check out.

Karla said, "I'll give you a dime." And the woman said, "No, it is the policy that makes me mad."

When the woman finally accepted the fact that she was not getting her seven cents back and stomped out of the store, it was Karla's turn. The associate was visibly emotionally disturbed at this encounter. In halting words, she almost whispered, "The last time this happened, I complained in our regional meeting, and they gave me the silent treatment. I'm sure my complaint is why I was denied the vacation dates I had requested."

Noting retaliation against an employee for questioning a policy makes other workers reluctant to speak the truth about other company issues they observe. Employees in a company may feel safe from physical bodily harm, but they may not feel safe emotionally, socially or psychologically. Consequently, Leadership Level 1 will only be effective when an organization truly embraces the concept of employees' total well-being.

Emotional Well-Being

Emotional well-being enables employees to effectively consider and work through their internal feelings and instinctual negative reactions to events in the workplace. In contrast to the retail clerk example mentioned above, workers require a safe environment for opening up about their questions and viewpoints on all issues that may seem incongruous or inappropriate to prevailing workplace attitudes. If workers do not feel safe to approach a topic, it delays the resolution of misconceptions. If workers try to address an issue and are met with criticism or contempt, communication barriers are built up. In this environment, emotional well-being declines.

When individuals muster the courage to divulge their flawed narrative and a manager or coworker points out the illogical part of the idea with contempt or scorn, the person feels rejected. They resist the new information and the viewpoint offered by the other person. Being dismayed by the rebuff of their ideas and equating it to rejection of them as a person, they retreat into a shell like a turtle and are reluctant to question other policies.

> Emotional well-being is tied to stress release, knowledge, and ability.

On the other hand, when a culture regularly and consistently evaluates differing viewpoints in a logical, rational, and unemotional process, it reduces employees' fear or reluctance to reveal their deeply-held concepts, notions and mindsets. They feel safe to surface the truth that is their reality. In this environment, erroneous, illogical, or faulty thinking is pointed out while maintaining the human dignity and emotional well-being of the individual.

Managers are not expected to go from boss to therapist, but they can help employees handle the stress of their jobs by recognizing their need for emotional well-being. When workers are mentally stressed and exhausted, problems arise. Every human has fears and anxieties about life's problems in addition to the angst about organizational issues and relationships.

It pays great dividends to be aware of the fears and anxieties employees are facing. Do they accept themselves as a worthy human being? Are they battling stress and burnout caused by company policies, practices, and culture? Are they fighting personal health challenges, financial or family problems? Check your absenteeism rates and insurance claims to assess this component of employee well-being in your organization.

Social Well-Being

Social well-being enables employees to deal with individual and workplace diversity stemming from a variety of educational, ethnic, and personality factors. There are many reasons coworkers feel uncomfortable around each other. Some reasons include being a new team member, lacking relationship building experiences, having different personality styles, values, needs, agendas, career goals, etc. Each of these reasons has a different resolution.

The previous factors that contribute to social discomfort are different than the reasons protected by law. Laws protect individuals from discrimination and harassment. Employees need an environment that is intolerant of online and in-person derogatory comments, verbal attacks, interpersonal intimidation,

> Being accepted by your group enhances social well-being.

bullying, and sexual harassment, both overt and covert. If people feel uncomfortable around others in their work environment because of any of these legal concerns, they are not in a socially safe place.

Social well-being requires an environment that recognizes diversity, accepts different personal values and welcomes ethnic cultures. Providing team-building and training opportunities so team members, managers, and coworkers get to know each other on more than a superficial level is an important strategy to promote social well-being.

Learning about the hidden motives that drive individuals and the various behavioral styles that cause conflict is the fundamental groundwork to help workers accept each other's strengths and limitations. This information paints a picture of an individual's uniqueness and contributes to the respect and human dignity required for social well-being. In Chapter 6, Social Acceptance, we explore this topic in more detail.

Psychological Well-Being

Running parallel to social and emotional well-being is psychological well-being. The term psychological well-being often includes acceptance by others and self-acceptance. A distinguishing feature in this discussion is the employee's ability to manage a complex company environment and make it harmonize with personal needs and values.

> Psychological well-being is having a measure of control over your life.

This requires space for autonomy of thought. Autonomy is self-rule or the freedom to think through and make decisions that affect an individual's personal future. It can be a monumental task to sort out what an employee can have control over and what needs to be yielded to the company, yet psychological well-being will be increased if the employees are given some level of autonomy over every possible facet of their assigned tasks.

Permitting employees freedom to organize their day, manage their environment to satisfy their personal needs, and regulate their personal schedule are important factors in psychological well-being. When managers look ahead and assign tasks in a reasonable time frame for completion and then step back, they make it possible for employees to have autonomy over their work days.

One additional factor in safety is to provide rational processes that follow logical procedures. In this process, employees should be safe to express their opinions as common-sense discussions unfold. Through the course of logical discussions, the person on the organizational chart who must make the final decision will make the final decision, but throughout the process, the employee should be permitted to have autonomy of thought and express those thoughts without incrimination.

Another form of psychological safety is that consequences, rewards, and decisions are administered objectively to all employees. Even though they have divergent opinions and are looking at situations through their own eyes, employees observe fairness. They should be confident that management has assessed and obsessed over what is fair for all. Fair for all should not be equated with equality. If decisions appear to be fair but unequal, the logic must be understood. Employees judge fairness by observing how peers, supervisors and subordinates are treated in comparison to their treatment and rewards. Anything less than equitable treatment causes an environment of distrust which erodes performance and employee loyalty to the organization.

By providing an environment that ensures the three qualities of well-being in addition to physical security for employees, Leadership Level 1 paves the way for employees to focus their discretionary effort on company goals and objectives.

The Practice of Discretionary Effort

Leadership of One Power Principle: Be the leader people choose to follow by creating a safe place.

Reflection

Safety and security are critical aspects of a healthy organization and they are intertwined with well-being. The opposite of well-being is *ill-being* which impedes discretionary energy. Organizations with highly developed safety and security programs promote physical health and well-being while reducing anxiety. When well-being is evident, organizational health is high and there is a positive flow of energy. When well-being is low, organizational vitality is inhibited and there is a negative drain on everyone in the organization.

Discretionary Effort Exercise:

Create a Safe Place

Survival is a fundamental instinct. We naturally work to ensure a safe environment, pay attention to what we are doing to avoid accidents, and look for unsafe circumstances around us. We operate as our own ongoing personal risk management team, adapting our behaviors and attitudes to our environment and circumstances to sustain our life as long as possible.

We also instinctively take care of others, responding to those who are in trouble or at risk with offers of physical help, advice and attention as we deem needed. Safety and security is a number one priority to preserve and sustain life.

Creating a safe place for yourself and others involves ensuring a nonviolent and nontoxic environment, paying attention to what you are doing, and being aware of the circumstances around you and your co-workers. The exercise for this chapter is to repeat "create a safe space" in your mind. This makes you aware of your surroundings from a different perspective than just checking off tasks during the day. Having a safe place forefront in your mind makes you more cautious as you perform routine tasks and helps you lookout for the best interests of your coworkers.

Discretionary Effort Practice Steps

Step 1: Observe and Experience. In the course of your day, be mindful of creating a safe place physically, emotionally and mentally. Be aware of your own feelings of well-being, the release of internal discretionary energy, and productivity.

Step 2: Contemplate and Record. Maintain a record of your experiences of creating a safe place.

Step 3: Share, Learn, and Model. After you have evaluated the following questions, share your insights and ask for input from a mentor, a friend, or trusted advisor.

1. What personal breakthroughs did I have about creating a safe place and well-being? Did I have any breakdowns when trying to create a safe space and improve well-being?
2. What breakthroughs or breakdowns did I note about safety and well-being in the organization?
3. What is the relationship between well-being and the release of discretionary effort?
4. How do I model creating a safe place physically, emotionally and mentally so that others also create space spots within the organization?

References

Drucker, P. (n.d.). Peter F. Drucker quotes. *Goodreads.com*. Retrieved from https://www.goodreads.com/author/quotes/12008.Peter_F_Drucker

Lee, J. P., Markowitz, K., Fahs, M., & Landrigan, P. (2000). *Costs of occupational injuries and illnesses*. Ann Arbor: University of Michigan Press.

Positioning Systems Blog. (2008, December 15). *Pearson's law*. Retrieved from http://positioningsystems.com/blog.php?entryID=67

United States Department of Labor. (n.d.). Safety and health add value. *Occupational Safety & Health Administration*. Retrieved from https://www.osha.gov/Publications/safety-health-addvalue.html.

Karla Brandau & Douglas Ross

CHAPTER 5

Looking Under the Hood at Safety

"At the end of the day, the goals are simple: safety and security."
~ Jodi Rell

If your vehicle needs oil, coolant, or you need to give the battery a charge, you immediately open the hood to expose the engine. In a similar way, this chapter looks under the hood of safety to determine if the company needs to keep going at a steady pace or if it needs a tune-up in order to speed up. Safety is at the heart of building the trust required for discretionary effort and is a bottom-up way to make sure the organization is looking out for every employee.

Doug learned a lesson about watching out for your coworkers, or "having their backs," in a very dramatic way. It was 8:32 p.m. and the maintenance staff had left at its regular time. The final station in an assembly line was jammed. Everyone knew the entire line had to shut down and the shift would be sent home without meeting their daily target.

The operator at the station and his supervisor had watched the maintenance crew repair this problem several times before. It was dangerous to fix the equipment, requiring advanced maintenance skill and necessitated strict safety procedures. Knowing the safety risks, the operator refused to try to correct the problem and called the shift supervisor, the senior person in the plant.

The shift supervisor was widely respected for doing what it took to meet daily targets. He was immersed in a culture of doing "whatever it takes." Even though he knew this was a dangerous situation, he took it upon himself to try to fix the problem. As soon as he assumed he had fixed the machine, it rumbled into action

75

without giving him time to get out of the way. The supervisor received fatal injuries.

His decision to risk safety in favor of meeting the shift's production goals led to disastrous consequences. Even though a federal investigation ruled his injuries an accident, everyone on the line knew otherwise. They knew the shift should have been sent home and the repairs given to the maintenance crew the next morning.

Leadership values are very influential in the level of risk-taking within an organization. How leaders react to safety issues makes an impression on how a workforce observes the safety rules and procedures. The attitude of upper management determines the organization's safety culture. When management creates an environment where quotas are the sole measure of performance, as in this company, the whatever-it-takes mentality makes this a repeatable story in other manufacturing and construction environments.

Fear and the Whatever-It-Takes Attitude

Albert Einstein said, "Three great forces rule the world: stupidity, fear and greed" (n.d.). These three forces can be found in every organization. Often, something stupid or unwise is said or done. Thus, individuals seek committees and teams to protect themselves from imprudent decisions. As to greed, there is a thin line between greed and the need to make a profit to stay in business. The line is difficult to distinguish because a profitable bottom-line is essential or the business will cease to exist.

Let's take a look at how the third quality of Einstein's three great forces – fear – impacts the release of discretionary effort inside people and organizations. What organizations and managers say may be very different than what they do "under the hood" as the saying goes. The Oxford Dictionary states that fear is one of the top 1,000 words used in UK English (n.d.). Fear is a negative emotion of anxiety caused by the threat of danger, pain, or harm. It is a strongly felt emotion that clouds rational thought and can be contagious in a company when used as a motivator.

In general, fear has a negative impact on job performance. While fear can be a temporary motivator, if leaders constantly use panic to accelerate performance, the results can be devastating. Under emotions of stress or terror, our minds lose the ability to use logic, focus, and planning skills so that the body can concentrate on the need for survival that is in the heart of every human being. The basic survival mechanism is called the General Adaptation Syndrome, where the body prepares to protect itself. In other words, fear activates the fight-or-flight response in humans and animals, and in this state of mind, workers will not make workplace safety a priority.

> Workers who routinely fear the loss of their job cannot focus on giving discretionary effort.

Continually dealing with the flight-or-fight syndrome destroys trust and alienates employees from the company. In a fearful environment, employees invest their discretionary time and effort ensuring personal defenses and protections, not improving products and services. Not only will employees spend their time watching out for danger, they will talk to others about their fears. Consequently, fear becomes contagious as mentioned above. Discretionary effort is negatively impacted, being eaten up by distress and anxiety in the organizational culture where it breeds.

Company Culture and Explicit vs. Implicit Rules

Organizational culture consists of the basic assumptions held by the individuals within an organization as a group. These assumptions are a mix of values, beliefs, meanings, and expectations. Group members hold many assumptions in common; they use them to judge what is acceptable behavior and problem-solving ideas.

Culture sets the tone for individual behavior in an organization. A negative culture, one of fear, undermines the effectiveness of the best programs, policies, and services intended to support the workforce. A culture of whatever-it-takes and profit-at-all-costs creates an environment of constant chaos and urgency where burnout is the norm.

Implementing Leadership Level 1 builds a positive culture as it addresses safety problems and focuses on the integrity of the organization's safety systems. Furthermore, a positive culture can move the organization into the upper stratosphere of financial stability and growth.

> Implicit rules are more powerful than explicit rules.

One of the 14 principles of quality stated by Edward Deming (2002), 20th century American management consultant, is that leadership needs to drive out fear, enabling everyone to work effectively for the company. A company culture of fear is usually established by implicit rules, such as in the do whatever-it-takes mentality, not explicit rules. Explicit means something that is clearly stated and formally expressed. Implicit is something that is understood but not expressed. Creating an implicit culture of fear is a short term success strategy that is counterproductive in the long term.

Even worse than being counterproductive, the implicit threat of being fired for not meeting targets sets the dangerous scene for excessive risk-taking. In a company where fear is a motivator, the explicit standard might be "safety first," but if it is implicitly accepted to do whatever-it-takes to meet goals and quotas, safety is compromised by workers who will risk anything for the deadlines. Once implicit threats and standards that negate safety are expelled, it is then possible to achieve the purpose of explicit safety standards: to keep the workplace free of recognized hazards that could cause death or serious physical harm to employees. Compliance with these rules is nonnegotiable and the implementation of the safety standards is a mutual responsibility of workers and management.

A simple example of explicit rules versus implicit culture is found in sick-day policies. In written communications and policies, a company might request that employees stay home with a cold or the flu in order to protect workers from communicable diseases. However, limiting sick days and failing to provide the technology necessary to work from home are company actions that implicitly encourage workers to come to the office when they are ill and more likely to spread influenza and cold germs.

A safety-conscious organization explicitly practices workplace safety systems and processes in the following ways:

- Specific training on safety procedures
- Direct and clear messaging in policy manuals
- Safety posters displayed throughout the plant, in the break room and lunchroom, and other places where they are highly visible
- Regular and consistent monitoring and evaluation of safety systems
- Discussions and company communications reminding employees of safety rules and goals

From Employee to Sherlock Holmes

In organizations, two distinct types of approaches for managing employees can be observed. First, there is a top-down approach, where management drives the process with supervisors measuring employee's behaviors and providing details in one-to-one feedback.

The second approach is bottom-up. This approach is an employee-driven process that encourages frontline participation in safety and security. It involves peer-to-peer observations and feedback to a team that makes recommendations to management for implementation.

The most effective results come from a combination approach. The ideal scenario is where the leadership team leads security initiatives but turns every employee into a Sherlock Holmes to relentlessly pursue safety issues. Just as employees walk through the company doors to give the organization eight hours or more of their brain and their brawn expecting to be safe, they should be expected to contribute to creating that secure environment. From a safety viewpoint it is important to come to each other's aid and protect each other from harm.

When workers pay attention to what is going on around them and find anything that is unsafe, they should be free to express their safety concerns without fear of repercussions. This applies even if a supervisor is breaking the rules just to stay on target for daily production goals.

In a human-led value culture, companies recruit employees to reduce injuries, illnesses and fatalities. Leaders listen and express gratitude for revealing safety concerns and the possible solutions individual employees offer. The employees become a resource as everyone works together to identify, resolve, and standardize safety systems. A common motto is, "Workplace safety begins with me."

> To ensure safety in the company, turn everyone into a Sherlock Holmes looking for potential dangers.

It must be noted that employees do not always respond correctly or promptly in dangerous situations and that employees learn through their mistakes. As a result of mistakes, organizations develop policies and procedures that standardize the reaction process to potential dangers. The standardization allows other employees to develop the knowledge and skills required to avoid accidents and unsafe conditions in the workplace.

Employee Involvement in Safety

The leaders of one company we interviewed told us of their program to reduce accidents. They guaranteed one personal day off (PTO) if the entire factory was accident-free for sixty days. The workers bonded together in an effort to reach this goal. They succeeded and as they moved into the second sixty-day experiment, a driver had an accident. Even though the driver was not a factory worker, every unit had to be accident free or no one received the PTO. The factory workers were demoralized and within one week after the driver's accident, the factory itself had an accident. This policy illustrates the power of rewards for safety, but it also warns how using rewards alone cannot guarantee long-term success.

Some companies have adopted a system where employees are expected to encourage each other's safety behaviors. It is a simple process using anonymous comment cards. Each employee receives two comment cards a week. The purpose of the card is to identify a fellow employee completing an operation safely.

The employees each receive a card, answer three questions about the operation being performed, and then take the time to acknowledge the specific protective actions the coworker completed. It is a wonderful system of recognition for demonstrating just how much energy employees will take to do the job safely and properly, instead of only expediently. Each card goes directly to the employee who is the subject of the review. Workers never know when they are being watched. It's another way employees ensure each other's safety using the observation skills of a Sherlock Holmes.

To further help turn employees into people who look after each other, implement the *Leadership of One Power Principle of Creating a Safe Space*. Through this principle, employees are involved in the decision-making process, so they can articulate and expose what is potentially dangerous. They expect that all accidents will be investigated with due diligence and that their security will not be held hostage by the pressure to increase production or meet deadlines.

Safety conscious, professionally minded workers—who, like Sherlock Holmes, are permitted to uncover the truth—create secure and productive work sites. If management attempts to step in and silence the voice of the employees, it may endanger the site, lose the respect of the workforce, and struggle to reverse the damage.

Some managers try to fix security hazards and lack of integrity in processes by firing a scapegoat. Firing a scapegoat is symbolic, not substantial. It doesn't work. For example, if something goes wrong, firing the director isn't the answer. Go to the delivery level of service and ask the people on the firing line: "Why aren't you doing it right?" "Why did this mistake happen?" When you get the answer, figure out what led the work culture to permit a mistake, then change that culture by empowering the workers to do what is right. An important final step is to pay employees well to do their jobs right and that includes funding to implement the right solution to fix safety hazards.

If you don't properly fund fixing the problem or pay employees enough to do the job well in a safe way, then employees will look for some way to "game the system," so it looks like they are getting their jobs done.

Gaming the System

When systems don't work and employees feel there is no other recourse, they will find a way to game the system. A game is a competitive activity played according to rules. Likewise, to game the system, employees engage three rules for their game:

- Management must not be aware the game is being played.
- The game must serve some practical purpose.
- While enjoyable, the game should have a relatively harmless impact on the bottom-line.

Employees shouldn't have to game the system to take care of their needs, but it happens in many organizations. For example, in a manufacturing facility with a multimillion-dollar lean production system, the employees learned that by putting a dime down on certain sensors in the system, they could shut the entire line down. They did this mostly to give themselves a break from the grueling schedule and to allow some line members to use the washroom facilities or to grab a quick snack. Every employee knew how long the line would be down. They had discovered all the sensors to stop the line and used them in a random fashion so as not to cause suspicion. In most of the cases, the management response team never even got around to problem-solving before the problem "resolved" on its own. Since all down time was in different locations involving different response teams, management never discovered the strategy.

Zero Accidents and Reality

There is one caution for leadership teams. If "zero accidents" is the deafening mantra of the leadership team, some departments will investigate every accident to learn how to better protect employees. Other departments will only report recordable accidents or even fudge the numbers or definitions of "accident" to obtain the goal of zero accidents. If the leadership team rewards the department that reported zero accidents because it had no "recordable" or "definable" accidents and punishes the department that took workplace safety seriously by reporting the minor accidents it investigated, then the integrity of the system is undermined.

In the example at the beginning of the chapter of the shift supervisor who lost his life in an attempt to keep on schedule, if the company had admitted fault, it would have cost them millions of dollars. By "covering it up" and not reporting the truth about the accident, they continued to win numerous safety awards. To this day, every employee knows the accident was covered up. A company that hides the truth cannot motivate employees to maintain a safe environment.

One company we researched was required to report spills to authorities. A conscientious manager reported every legal spill to the authorities. When the authorities sought to shut the company down, the company fired the manager and replaced him with another department manager who had no spills on his record. Why no spills? He didn't report them. Not reporting spills keeps the company in business but the employees know the spills are being covered up. Again, these employees know they do not work in a safe environment, so it is unlikely that they will make safety a priority.

When posters and explicit rules state: "Safety is the first priority," but the priorities of the implicit workplace are skewed in favor of production, not compliance, employees know. If safety structures are geared toward protecting the company from health and safety legislation, then the company will do whatever is necessary to show statistics indicating they are following the law. However, when a choice has to be made between safety and production, employees know the implicit rule is to sacrifice safety. In this environment, workers protect themselves in any way they can from personal injury or being held liable for an accident. Their discretionary effort is focused on minimizing their risk, not on adding value to the process or the product.

Employees, understanding the explicit rationale for all systems and processes, look for the essence, the implicit truth in the company culture. With trepidation, they ask the question "Is the company really looking after my safety?"

The Practice of Discretionary Effort

LEADERSHIP OF ONE
POWERFUL PRINCIPLE

Leadership of One Power Principle: Be the leader people choose to follow— validate what is right and work to be error free.

Reflection

Being human is admitting the truth that we are not perfect and neither are our coworkers or direct reports. When we admit we are mortal with weaknesses and limitations, we can work on reducing human errors, workplace incidents, and stress. Aligning explicit rules of safety with the implicit social contract that is part of a human-led value system is the first step in doing the right things and reducing human errors. Let's suppose the explicit rules of the company are about teamwork and collaboration. However, the implicit rule states that selfish people advance faster. If the explicit and implicit rules don't match, employees will never become the eyes and ears of the organization or reveal new ways of preventing mistakes and human errors.

Discretionary Effort Exercise:

Validate What Is Right and Work to Be Mistake Free

Acknowledging and being grateful for good work is an effective way to motivate employees. People like to be recognized for what they do that is right. The recognition encourages them to find new ways to make value added contributions or give discretionary effort. Ironically, you need to validate what employees do well but encourage them to identify flaws in the workplace. When personnel find what is wrong and work to be mistake free, the workplace is safer, the quality is higher, and the number of customer complaints is more likely to decrease.

Recognize that we will never completely eradicate human errors. Then repeat to yourself, "Validate what is right and work to be mistake free." The result is gratitude for the successes and clarity to foresee errors. Don't wait until after mistakes are made before you look for a solution. As the legendary basketball coach John Wooden is attributed as saying: If you don't have time to do it right the first time, when will you have time to do it over?

Discretionary Effort Practice Steps

Step 1: Observe and Experience. In the course of the day, be mindful of reducing human errors: both your own and the mistakes of others. Did you observe positive benefits of acknowledging that humans make mistakes? What are the unintended consequences that can and do arise because of human frailty?

Step 2: Contemplate and Record. Maintain a record of your experiences of working to eliminate human errors.

Step 3: Share, Learn and Model. After you have evaluated the following questions, share your insights and ask for input from a mentor, a friend, or a trusted advisor.

1. What personal breakthroughs did I experience by evaluating my propensity to human errors and how to avoid them? Did I experience any breakdowns or errors that could have been avoided?
2. Did I observe errors and mistakes made by others that could have been avoided?
3. What is the relationship between admitting I am human, making mistakes, correcting my mistakes, and increasing my discretionary energy?
4. How can I constructively model how to handle errors in a way that releases discretionary effort?

References

Deming, W. E. (2002). *Out of the crisis*. Cambridge: Massachusetts Institute of Technology, Center for Advanced Engineering Study.

Einstein, A. (n.d.). *Goodreads.com*. Retrieved from http://www.goodreads.com/quotes/261845-three-great-forces-rule-the-world-stupidity-fear-and-greed

Fear. (n.d.). In Oxford dictionaries online. *Oxford University Press*. Retrieved from http://www.oxforddictionaries.com/us/definition/american_english/fear

CHAPTER 6

Leadership Level 2:
Social Acceptance

"People will forget what you said, forget what you did, but people will never forget how you made them feel."
~ Maya Angelou

Figure 6.1: Leadership Level 2, Social Acceptance

Once employees feel safe and secure in the company's office building and perceive the company cares about their well-being, they move to Level Two on the Discretionary Effort pyramid, Social Acceptance. They look to their manager and their team members to find acceptance as individuals.

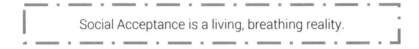

Social Acceptance is a living, breathing reality.

Each employee contributes to the social environment. As people move in and out of the company, the social environment changes which explains why Leadership Level 2, Social Acceptance, illustrated in Figure 6.1, involves living, breathing assets and is central to the health of the organization. Creating a company culture that moves and stretches to people's personalities and strengths provides a huge opportunity for organizational stability.

All people crave to be respected and accepted for their authentic identities and inherent traits. When employees are socially accepted and recognized in positive ways, they are free to focus their energies on solving problems, not worrying about bodily or psychological harm or personal rejection. Social acceptance removes fear, promotes stability, and frees employees to be top performers.

The Heart of the Company

People are at the heart of all things that work in the company. In fact, through their acquisition of knowledge and application of personal insight, they are the only asset that gains value over the years.

Leaders who take care of the heart of their company, the people, offer acceptance and respect to each employee. As employees are offered social acceptance and respect as an individual, the company becomes people-centered, creating a human-led value culture as opposed to an operational-led culture.

As your employees interact and relate in meaningful ways, their social interactions become windows where observers can view the heart and soul of the organization. As people look in through the windows, they can see immediately how people behave toward others and interact with each other translates into organizational health and well-being or dysfunction and chaos.

Doug had an experience that dramatically proves this point. When Doug was consulting with one Japanese manufacturing company, he was asked to evaluate a problem on the line. The management had lined up people for him to interview, but Doug wanted to talk to people management had not designated available for conversations—people Doug thought might be the actual heart of the company.

As he walked through the factory, he saw the line was down and stopped to talk to one of the workers on the floor. Doug asked him a couple of simple questions, and it became very apparent that he was dissatisfied with the company. He didn't give Doug any specifics, so Doug reasoned the dissatisfaction could have arisen from the man's attitude and not necessarily from a flaw inside the company.

However, Doug was abruptly interrupted by the employee's supervisor who politely reprimanded him for interfering with the production system. He implied that Doug had distracted the employee, causing him to take his eye off his very important job and resulting in the shutdown of the line.

> People are the only asset that does not depreciate but gains value over the years.

This was insulting to Doug because the allegation was untrue. Doug hadn't stopped the employee to talk; he talked with the employee because the line had stopped. If the supervisor had not made a personal attack, Doug probably would have given the company the benefit of the doubt, but now Doug knew he had uncovered a partial truth about the company's management style. He would not have known this if he had not spoken to someone not on the list of employees designated for interviewing. By that chance conversation, Doug saw more clearly through the window into the chaos at the company.

Human Dignity

At the root of Leadership Level 2 and the release of discretionary effort is the principle of human dignity. When you embrace human dignity as a platform to achieve increased performance, then valuing every person in the organization and creating a human-led value culture becomes part of your ethos as a leader. You see the fundamental significance of everyone in the organization.

> "I speak to everyone in the same way, whether he is the garbage man or the president of the university."
> ~ Albert Einstein

Human dignity is a fundamental value. It is a basic ethical and legal principle throughout the world. Human dignity is a principle that is part of everything from hiring and firing, to disabilities, civil rights, and seeing inequalities. It is recognizing respect for the inherent and immeasurable worth of every human being. To truly recognize human dignity, it is crucial to look at others from various places or cultures, whose beliefs may seem unusual, and still offer sincere respect.

When human dignity is a fundamental value at your company, your leadership team will offer authentic human developmental opportunities to your employees. The question you must ask is "How well do my managers respect the human dignity of employees at every level of my organization?"

Social Acceptance

Social acceptance can be achieved in two ways. First, everyone must conform to the group. In order to fit in with others, most people will adapt to look and act like those around them. In other words, the individual sacrifices parts of his or her identity in order to be accepted as "one of the crowd." Second, the group must learn to accept or tolerate different and diverse individuals.

Blending In

For most people, being part of the crowd is a basic human need. It is good to belong to something bigger than one's self. There is something fulfilling in belonging to a purposeful group in motion. When people feel welcome, wanted, and worthy in a company environment, this social acceptance increases work production both individually and collectively.

The issue with being one of the crowd or blending in is that some people have difficulty fitting the mold. They lack the ability to look and act like everyone else. These employees often do not feel welcome, wanted and worthy. In some strange way they may appear to blend in as a member of the group, but at the core, they do not socially interact with the group. This is particularly difficult for them when there are several sub-groups within the whole company.

> People often have to choose whether to blend in and become one of the crowd or maintain a portion of their individuality.

Faced with the reality that they are not one of the crowd, many employees choose to stay with the organization and do the work they are paid to do. They have chosen to accept themselves and their situational reality: they may not fit within the group, but they simply are part of the group by virtue of membership in the organization.

With this mature attitude, these individuals recognize all the good and bad parts in the existing workplace without wanting to change or fix it. They are happy with who they are. They appreciate, validate, accept, and support their independence, while understanding their need to be part of a group. In some organizations, acceptance or blending in is an either-or situation; either you are in or you are out. It is a credit to the company that can make employees feel welcome, wanted, and worthy even though they don't fit the most prevalent mold of employee.

Accepting Differences

Organizations that reject the in-or-out scenario opt for the second type of social acceptance: the ability to recognize, then tolerate or embrace differences. When the diverse characteristics of individual employees are looked upon as a strength, then ideas and solutions are coalesced from a wide range of cultural and educational experiences the diverse employees bring to the table.

The social acceptance of diversity maximizes the interactions and collaboration between team members. In a culture of social acceptance, every employee senses the need to interact with, learn about, relate to and build friendships with diverse coworkers at every level of the organization. As a final note, from an individual viewpoint, true social acceptance also involves high self-esteem and the commitment to be both part of the group while remaining uniquely authentic.

Accept the Entire Package

The employee is an entire package: strengths and limitations. Social acceptance means each individual is accepted *as is*. Similar to shopping in the scratch and dent section of an appliance store and choosing a washer with a dent in the side, you accept the washer *as is*. You know that you can put the dent against the wall, no one will ever see it, and you will get great value for your money.

As you accept employees for their strengths and what they can contribute, you get great value for your hire. Along with accepting their incredible strengths, you must also accept that every employee comes with a few blind spots and limitations that create gaps in performance. For instance, some individuals excel at creating ideas but are not good at laying out a plan for implementation. Some employees shine at seeing the future but do not have the ability to learn from past mistakes. Other employees are good at picking

> It is important to accept every individual "as is" and then help them grow professionally.

things apart and analyzing problems but have no clue how to build consensus.

Leaders who successfully implement Leadership Level 2 get to know their employees so well that they understand their strengths and can intuitively give them stewardship over projects and tasks where they can surpass expectations. They pair employees with complementary strengths for the best project team, such as pairing an employee with creative big picture skills with a team member who is detail oriented and can execute the implementation plan.

Human Idiosyncrasies and Full Potential

Acceptance does not mean that everything employees do is correct and right and that every decision will be the right decision. Bill Gates once said, "How a company deals with mistakes suggests how well it will wring the best ideas and talents out of its people."

There will be mistakes. If they make a human error or their innovative project flops, employees need to know there will not be drastic repercussions and they will not be fired as discussed in Chapter 5. When superior relationships exist, managers forgive human errors and encourage risk taking.

> Accepting an individual "as is" does not mean tolerating bad behavior or not holding them accountable.

Acceptance as is does not mean denying or excusing away bad behavior. Human idiosyncrasies and personality limitations can be quite messy at times. Do not confuse acceptance and respect with tolerance for poor performance.

Tolerance of bad behaviors breeds negative feelings about the poorly performing employee and feeds the negative gossip in a company. The negative feelings may be suppressed in conversations in meetings but are evident through body language, tone of voice, and attitude toward the employee that surface. Rather than tolerating bad behaviors and destroying the camaraderie of social acceptance, strong leaders have honest conversations with any employee whose performance is below standard. They look for root causes for the bad behavior then work to coach and mentor the employee to new levels of performance. Strong leaders state the expected standards and set up a personal growth path for the challenged employee. They do not settle for mediocre contributions from any worker.

Having the courage to hold people accountable for their actions and relentlessly encouraging greater competence means initiating difficult conversations with the employee and identifying a path forward to improved performance. Done in the right spirit, this process can forever change the employee's future.

On the other side of the coin, the individual who wants to reach their full potential must follow the path of aggressive professional growth. Employees should seek self-knowledge and work to improve their personal limitations through constant improvement of their knowledge and skills.

Marcus Buckingham and Donald Clifton (2010) in *Now Discover Your Strengths*, recommend that organizations identify the strengths and limitations of employees and coach them to improve their limitations only to the point where those boundaries are no longer liabilities. This is in stark contrast to training programs where the goal is to make a limitation a strength. Individuals who focus on their strengths build even greater aptitudes and the ability to provide exceptional performances on a daily basis (Sorenson 2014). This approach makes a great deal of sense. Organizations that constantly try to improve the limitations and liabilities of employees may be missing stellar performances that are an outgrowth of their strengths.

Managers often deliver passionate pep talks, overdose employees on guilt, give long lectures, resort to threats, and other types of verbal gymnastics to get employees to overcome their limitations. However, the best way to decrease limitations and magnify strengths is to establish superior relationships, drive out fear, and proactively plan personal growth with the employee.

Acknowledgment as Motivation

Skilled leaders can expect discretionary effort from employees who understand how mundane tasks—like completing an audit, hammering a nail, or making a difficult phone call—leads to the success of the company. Perhaps more important than the knowledge of what their job adds to the company is acknowledgement of their personal contribution.

Studies consistently show that compensation is overestimated as a motivational tool. It ranks third or fourth as a tool for motivating job performance. Rather than money, individuals are motivated on an emotional level by acceptance, recognition, and empathy. Companies should require high production quality, but sometimes their efforts to achieve optimum output comes at the expense of what motivates their employees on an emotional level.

For instance, when there is a problem on a manufacturing line, a company might bring in their quality engineers who proceed through a process designed to identify and resolve the problem. If they conduct their assessment by excluding the people on the line, they demotivate the line employees and lose the opportunity to gain valuable insights from their tactical, hands-on knowledge.

> Acknowledgement of employee contributions is a powerful motivational force.

As an example, when Doug was working with a very large world-wide financial organization, their entire internet service went down for a couple of hours costing them millions of dollars. By accident, Doug met one of the key programmers who was widely known as brilliant but lacking in personality and tact. Doug asked him about the problem, and the programmer said he had informed management of the potential outage months ago, but they refused to listen, which had made him very angry.

His overreaction to the incident resulted in a negative write-up. He went on to say that because of their response, he stopped telling them about the issue, and now they had discovered it themselves. It was an expensive lesson that need not have happened if they had only acknowledged the programmer's expertise and paid him the highest compliment: listening to his warning and implementing his remedy.

In contrast, Karla recounts a positive illustration of a leader who used acknowledgement in the correct way. We'll call the manager Kari. Kari managed 65 nurses in a well-respected hospital. They delivered stellar customer service and patient care even through personal challenges.

One personal challenge occurred when a nurse inadvertently injected herself with blood from a known HIV patient. While other nurses may have been too emotionally upset to continue, this nurse rose to the challenge and continued to care for her patients until she was relieved by another nurse. Kari went out of her way to ensure this nurse received the proper treatment.

On the same shift, another nurse received a call to pick up her very sick child from school. Kari was supportive and immediately called in another nurse to finish the shift. Until the replacement arrived, the nurse continued with her duties, fully focused on her patients while she waited for her colleague.

The next day when an unexpected snowstorm hit, another nurse drove through the heavy snow to get to the hospital because she did not want to leave her patients without care. Knowing she would probably be snowed in at the hospital for a while, she brought a couple of changes of clothes.

> Be aware of the personal sacrifices employees make to ensure their work is completed.

As an experienced and intuitive leader, Kari showed great empathy for the work of her nurses as they delivered professional care in spite of their personal challenges and in spite of being asked to work overtime. The next week at the employee luncheon, Kari recognized each nurse who had dealt with a problem and acknowledged the nurses who worked overtime to cover for them. Kari verbalized her gratitude, spoke about their dedication and sacrifice, and affirmed them as individuals. She named each employee specifically and thanked them. It was obvious the nurses were moved.

As a leader seeking to establish superior relationships with your workers, ask yourself: "What price have my people paid? What have they sacrificed? Have I thanked them? Can I put myself in their place and feel what they feel?" Acknowledging the sacrifice employees give connects managers and employees in a profound way.

Next, acknowledge their effort. To self-evaluate, when was the last time you sent a thank-you note to a team member mentioning the excellent customer service you observed? When was the last time you stopped at someone's desk and personally thanked them for a report that was thorough and professional? Have you ever thanked the spouse or partner of an employee who worked the weekend?

These small acts of gratitude matter more than you can imagine. They improve morale, engage the heart and deepen the feeling of social acceptance.

Social Acceptance Strategies

Social acceptance is the foundation of employee engagement, employee appreciation, and the earning of discretionary effort. The four simple rules of social acceptance are:

1. **Involve your employees in planning at every stage of company development.** People take personal ownership of what they create, from the company mission statement to quarterly production goals; workers are an untapped resource of ideas.

2. **Make social acceptance a strategy that infiltrates the entire company, not just a program.** A program has a beginning and an end. A strategy is ongoing, dynamic, and changes as needed. Employees don't stick around companies hoping to get the Employee of the Month or a 10-year service award. Employees stay because they feel accepted, valued, and appreciated for their day-to-day contributions. Train every manager and supervisor in how to give personal recognition to each employee under their stewardship so recognition and engagement are daily actions. If recognition is established as a daily routine, then it

will less likely get pushed to the next day, week, month, or year.

3. **Recognize risk takers, promote initiative, and give verbal credit when their suggestions are implemented.** Seeing their ideas in practice gives employees a feeling of pride and accomplishment. Recognition is the best reward of all.

4. **Pull the diverse elements of your social groups together by continually painting a vivid picture of a better tomorrow and demonstrating how employees can be optimistic in the face of sometimes formidable odds.** Employees who are embroiled in day-to-day battles for market share, getting the product to market, or fixing the flaws in a software program become oblivious to the overall missions and objectives of the company. Communicate the overall vision in constant sound bites of "This is our goal; this is why we do this; this is our vision." These subtle reminders to see the big picture keep employees focused on the future, feeling part of the group, and knowing they are needed instead of being dragged down by the daily grind of meeting deadlines.

As you implement these four rules for social acceptance and engagement you will be building a great workplace that attracts and keeps talented employees who give discretionary effort on a daily basis.

The Practice of Discretionary Effort

LEADERSHIP OF ONE
POWERFUL PRINCIPLE

Leadership of One Power Principle: Be the leader people choose to follow by accepting what is at the present moment as the starting point for change and transformation.

Reflection

Through their acquisition of knowledge and application of personal insight and wisdom, employees are the only assets that gain value over time. Individually, employees gain in value as they grow professionally. As knowledge is shared and teams learn together, the entire workforce likewise gains value through the weeks and months of working together. To quote an often used phrase— business moves at the speed of relationships. The purpose of a strategy of social acceptance is to build superior relationships that release discretionary effort in workers at all levels of the organization.

A strategy of social acceptance is built on the principle of human dignity and the right of every person to add value to products and services through their innate character gifts. The RossBrandau Leadership Model advocates the recognition of human dignity and human potential in order to help employees accept their personal dignity and be held accountable for their professional growth.

Social acceptance enhances well-being and enables managers to handle human mistakes and errors in a fair way that emphasizes solutions. The environment of social acceptance results in a more productive, collaborative, creative, and inclusive workplace.

Discretionary Effort Exercise:

Accept What Is, As It Is, In the Present Moment

Social acceptance refers to the ability to accept or to tolerate differences and diversity in other people or groups of people. Acceptance is the first step in transformation. In order to experience social acceptance and the resulting discretionary energy, what is happening at the present moment must first be accepted. Then it can be rationally and intellectually evaluated and improved.

Accepting your strengths and limitations and assessing the reality and truth about what you do, think, and say leads you to personal change. It is important to understand that looking for the truth in your actions does not mean judging or criticizing yourself. It means simply accepting things as they are. For example, if you are a manger and you make a mistake, admit it and look for a solution. The admission of mistakes allows leaders to correct the situation instead of denying, hiding and suppressing what happened. This creates a culture of action and solving problems to move forward.

Saying "Accept what is as it is" repeatedly in your mind allows you to accept the actions of others and yourself as a beginning point in transformation. In order to get to where you want to go, you must first accept where you are.

Discretionary Effort Practice Steps

Step 1: Observe and Experience. In the course of your day be mindful of whether or not you are accepting people and events as they are. As the praxis assignment is repeated in daily relationships, ask yourself, "Am I accepting things as they are? Can I be the change I want in this organization. Can I accept other people as is? Can we accept what is and then move forward to transformational change?"

Step 2: Contemplate and Record. Maintain a record of your experiences of acceptance as your personal transformation process to acquire more discretionary effort through the release of your personal gifts of character, insight, and skills.

Step 3: Share, Learn, and Model. After you have evaluated the following questions, share your insights and ask for input from a mentor, a friend or trusted advisor.

1. What personal breakthroughs did I have when accepting myself? Did I experience any breakdowns when accepting my strengths and limitations?
2. Do others in the organization recognize and accept what is as it is and a starting point for improvement?
3. What is the relationship between acceptance and discretionary effort?
4. How can I model acceptance for organization processes and people in the organization as a

starting place for moving forward so that others
will follow my example?

References

Buckingham, M. & Clifton, D. O. (2001). Now discover your
strengths. NY: Free Press.

Sorenson, S. (2014, February 20). How employees' strengths make
your company stronger. *Business Journal*. Retrieved from
http://www.gallup.com/businessjournal/167462/employees-
strengths-company-stronger.aspx

CHAPTER 7

The 20th Century Social Contract

"I think the game has changed—we are emerging from an era of
operational-led value (the mantra of industrialized manufacturing)
to one of human-led value (innovation, creativity, life solutions,
services) where growing the right people will grow the business,
connect communities and do better for the world."
~ *Vincent Tuckwood*

An operational-led value social contract focuses energy on defining
separate and distinct concepts such as quality, efficiency, and safety
in order to measure durability, throughput, accidents and
profitability as part of a process. The total focus is on measurement
of processes and the identification of value added elements that
are quantifiable. Humans in this
contract make themselves
available for work according to an
explicit contract that is agreed
upon by both parties. An
important point is that workers in
an operational-led value system
are dispensable for growth.

> The operational-led social
> contract is valuable, but the
> human-led social contract
> is invaluable. Organizations
> need both, not one or the
> other.

A human-led value social
contract focuses energy on
releasing discretionary effort in solution-oriented problem solving
and in the development of innovative new products that benefit the
customer. Workers in this contract freely give discretionary effort
according to an implicit social contract that recognizes their value-
added contributions. In a human-led value system, workers are
indispensable for growth and economic sustainability.

The best way to illustrate the difference is the approach to profitability. An operational-led social contract values questions such as "How can we get more money from customers?" or "How can we reduce our costs?" A human-led social contract values questions such as "How can we provide product and service innovation that benefits our customers?"

The operational-led value social contract is important, but the human-led social contract is invaluable. Organizations need both, not one or the other.

Understanding Social Contracts

The business dictionary defines a social contract as "unwritten and tacit agreement said to exist among the member of a community or group that guides individual behavior and establishes personal rights and responsibilities." In every company there is a social contract that is implicit, or implied but not plainly expressed. The implicit social contract is unseen but none-the-less is more powerful than the explicit, formal contract signed when hired.

In the same way as there are consequences to breaking the explicit contract of organizational policies and procedures, there are consequences for non-conformance to the social contract. Being ostracized from the group is an example of non-conformance to the social contract.

To better understand the role social acceptance plays in the 21st century, an examination of social contracts and the 20th century implicit social contract is warranted. From the beginning of time, contracts have been associated with work—even if the parties involved didn't know what a contract was. The first contract may have been when the cavewoman said to her caveman, "If you go hunt a saber-toothed tiger, I will skin it, cut it up, and cook it for you when you get back."

Before examining how the 21st century social contract at work evolved, three questions need to be answered: Why is work essential? Why do we work? And what is work? The answers to these questions provide insight into the evolution of social contracts in companies.

Why Work Is Essential

At its very core, work is essential to human beings. It is an indispensable part of life for everyone on earth. A day filled with meaningful work feeds the human psyche with feelings of self-esteem. From the beginning, families were responsible for their own survival. As a family, they performed every task collectively for their existence. Together they hunted, farmed, built, sewed, cooked, cleaned, and cleared the land. One day someone noticed that a neighboring family was better at farming than building and decided to barter with them. "If we grow extra food and give it to you, will you build a couple of extra rooms onto the house we live in?"

An understanding of the exchange of work was born. Both families benefited from the arrangement: Better food was grown and stronger homes were built. In the end, individuals were able to pursue meaningful work and contribute to society using their gifts, skills, and talents.

Over the decades the exchange of work evolved from trading services and talents to trading skills and effort for money. This enabled people to move beyond "working to live" to "living a life" that included enhanced aspects of living such as travel, vacations, hobbies, sports, theatre and education.

> Work is essential for personal sustainability, for self-worth and for self-actualization.

In spite of increased opportunities, living a life still eludes some. Many employees put in eight hours every day just to pay for the cost of living. Others work eight hours a day doing work that has little meaning for them personally. They work merely for the freedom of retirement. Even though each group works hard, their gifts and talents may not be fully used, some even untapped. When gifts and talents are not developed, both the company and the individual miss the benefits of value added contributions and the giving of discretionary effort. In an environment where gifts and talents are untapped and lay latent, work often loses meaning to the employee, contributing to dwindling energy and burn out for the employee.

In *The Why of Work: How Great Leaders Build Abundant Organizations That Win*, Dave Ulrich and Wendy Ulrich (2010) summarize why employees need to have meaning at work:

> "Even if you are not one of those rare folks blessed with a gift for finding joy in the concentration camps of life, you intuitively know that you and your work team would be more productive, more satisfied, and more creative if work engaged not only your head and your hands but your heart and soul as well. What most of us know intuitively research confirms: When employees find meaning at work, they care enough about it to develop their competence; they work harder and are more productive; they stay longer and are more positive about their work experience. But there is more: When employees are more positive, customers generally respond in kind. Employee attitude is a key lead indicator of customer attitude, and satisfied customers help the businesses they patronize to survive and thrive."

In other words, in spite of an individual's preoccupation with personal needs and dreams, work still is the place where meaning is achieved. It is through work that potential and self-actualization are realized, even if the individual is unaware of what is happening.

Why Do We Work?

We work to earn a living. The work ethic should start early in the home as children are given chores. The work ethic is perfected in 12-20 years of schooling. The repeated message is work hard, be good, obey authority, pay attention, study, specialize, grow, learn, and you will be a success in life. After schooling, the mantra becomes a way of life as we work hard, obey company rules, support leadership, achieve results, grow the business, and enjoy a wealth of success in the work world. The people who follow this mantra usually do well and earn enough money not only to survive but also to live an enriched lifestyle and enjoy a comfortable retirement.

> For self-fulfillment, the work you do on a daily basis needs to have meaning and give you satisfaction. Fulfillment is essential for personal sustainability, self-worth and self-actualization.

The philosophy becomes convoluted when financial accomplishments become the only measurement of success. A fundamental truth is that once you earn enough to pay for the cost of living, success takes on other dimensions. More money does not necessarily translate into a happy life nor a life well lived. People without surplus money do survive and are often very happy as money is not their only measurement of success. Many are happy with a comfortable but small retirement home. Others enjoy children and extended family as a measure of their happiness and success.

Life-style choices are reflected in Abraham Maslow's Hierarchy of Human Needs. According to Maslow, first, work ensures basic biological and physiological needs are met—food, water, shelter, etc. Once these needs are met, we progress to having safety needs met. We need laws and order in society to provide safety and we pay for these needs through taxes.

At the next level, we want to love and belong. Many try but find that money can't buy the fulfillment of the need for acceptance. As we are satisfied in our relationships, we move to the fourth level: building self-esteem. Again, money is not an assurance that we will meet a high level of esteem. As self-esteem needs are met, we look for self-actualization and adding value to lives of those around us. Self-actualization can take a life time and can be tied to work, hobbies, or passions, such as running marathons or helping third world countries battle disease and poverty.

The work we do to earn a living should be fulfilling but it is important to admit that every job contains some dull and routine work. Karla has taught time management to thousands of people in her career and one of her proprietary principles is this: You must enjoy 80 percent of your job. If you can enjoy 80 percent of what you do, don't give emotional energy to the 20 percent you don't like. Delegate or dispose of the tasks you don't like in the most efficient way possible. When managers and individuals understand the

80/20 balance, stress is reduced and employees are encouraged to give discretionary effort to the 80% of tasks that are prioritized as the most important.

What Is Work?

Work is performing a job or a task. Work takes energy. In science, energy or effort is defined as the ability to do work. It is the physical or mental energy that is exerted in order to achieve a purpose. In this discussion, work is energy expended by an individual and transferred to a task, transforming the task into a valuable entity.

In physics, work is defined as force times distance (f x d). Work becomes the force applied to overcome resistance and inertia. As you apply force, you overcome inertia, prevent stagnation, and make work move forward. Physics attaches another term to the measure of work: a joule (pronounced "jewel"). In organizations, people are the force that overcomes inertia, and the discretionary effort they bring is the jewel.

The stronger the force, the higher the energy and the more work is done. In this context, it makes sense that the organization seeks to move employees to higher levels of energy. As employees move to higher levels of energy, their jewels of discretionary effort are released. Their effort contributes to the explicit and implicit understanding that forms the organization's social contract that governs the behaviors demonstrated in the organization.

Capitalism and Social Contracts

Capitalism is a social system based on the principle of individual rights. These rights are embodied in the social contract. The social contract manifests the nature of the exchanged value between the individual's work and the organization's profits. It is a delicate balance between the amount

> Discretionary effort overcomes inertia and is the "jewel" workers give your company.

of freedom a person has to do the assigned work and the policies and procedures of the organization.

The most fundamental right is the unalienable right to life. The rights to liberty, property, and the pursuit of happiness are derived from the right to life. The organization should honor and respect the individual's inalienable rights of life and liberty just as the individual should respect the inalienable rights of the organization to prosper in a competitive marketplace.

Each party in the agreement has the free will to choose whether or not to enter into a contractual relationship and has the right to negotiate the elements of the contract. The contract must be mutually beneficial and either party is free to renegotiate any part deemed to be unequal or unfair.

Contracts, Social Contracts, and Work

In the 21st century, work is not about trading home-grown vegetables for cutting lumber to build a house. For the past two centuries, work has involved two entities: an employer and an employee. Between the two entities, there are two kinds of contracts: legal (an explicit contract) and social (an implicit contract), which is synonymous with organizational culture.

The legal contract is the hard copy, signed contract that explicitly details what the employee must do to receive a pay check. For example, a signed legal contract states, "You get paid ten dollars an hour." If the employee receives a paycheck that week and gets five dollars an hour, a legal issue exists because of the discrepancy between the payment and the explicit agreement.

> There is a difference in explicit, legal contracts and implicit social contracts.

Then there is an understanding, an implicit agreement, or a social contract about what the employer will provide in return for an employee coming to work every day. Employees are given a work area, work equipment, software appropriate for their job, training, a lunch hour and regular breaks. This unwritten social contract has ramifications every hour of the day and is intertwined with employee motivation.

When engagement and the giving of discretionary effort come into play, as per the implicit social contract, employees expect that if they work exceptionally hard, in return, they will receive some additional compensation. Compensation from the employer could be a monetary bonus, an "Employee of the Month" plaque, or a company coffee mug. Whatever the reward, it is an expected part of the social contract.

Although the expected reward might be different today than it was in the past, implicit and explicit contracts, are not modern phenomena. In the agrarian economy, the explicit contract sealed by a handshake was, "I will pay you 25 cents per day and you will remove this stump from my field." The implicit agreement was, "I will give you an honest day's pay for an honest day's work."

What motivated an employee in this era? Honor and individual character. In that century, the worker's family name may have been the only thing passed down to him, and he didn't want to be the one that ruined it for the entire family. Maintaining your family reputation was intrinsic motivation.

As time passed, the explicit work contract before World War II was, "I will pay you an agreed-upon amount of money. You will work the agreed-upon number of hours per day." The pre-World War II implicit social contract was: "I will manage you and tell you exactly what to do. You will do precisely what I prescribe."

What motivated the pre-World War II employee? Fear. Employees were just a number without consideration given to pensions, health care plans or sick leave. The explicit motivation was for employees to follow explicit rules or be fired. If you were a worker, you didn't need to engage your brain. Management would do the thinking for you.

Post-World War II explicit contracts did not vary much from pre-World War II: "I will pay you an agreed-upon amount of money. You will work the agreed-upon number of hours per day." Except management added: "I will pay you extra for overtime." This was the first time that employees could potentially define their own destiny by electing to work extra hours to make additional money. The post-World War II implicit or social contract was: "You will have an office, proper equipment, time at the water cooler, and free coffee."

What motivated these employees? Being able to build a big house for their family of 2.5 kids, with a tire swing out front, and a white picket fence. Another prominent feature after World War II was the military form of management embraced by organizations which mirrored the distinctions between enlisted men and officers. This mimicked the pre-World War II world where the lines were clear between workers and management.

This philosophy of the divisions between management and workers was postulated by Frederick Winslow Taylor in his book *Principles of Scientific Management*, first printed in 1911. His theories, known as Taylorism, were introduced at the beginning of the 20th century to increase the productivity of workers laboring in factories.

Taylor (2012) advocated the benefits of redesigning work to wrest control from workers and place it in the hands of management. He promoted the idea that some people should be paid to think and others paid to labor. Taylorism argued that the separation of thought from execution would strengthen the division between managers—whose job was to think and design—and workers—whose job it was to follow instructions.

> The separation of thought from execution fostered distrust between management and workers.

This fostered division between the so-called white-collar and blue-collar jobs. As the first factories followed Taylor's philosophies, there was no attempt to create meaningful work for employees. Workers took on thankless jobs, unforgiving schedules, and often suffered demeaning language. Management expected workers to perform as fast as humanly possible to complete mindless tasks. Distrust and hostility between workers and their bosses was the result. Engagement and discretionary effort were non-existent.

The philosophies of Taylorism began to be questioned in the 1940's. Taylorism was no longer able to motivate workers and managers looked for new ways to stimulate people to meet production quotas. As the world shifted from factory to office jobs, the philosophies of Abraham H. Maslow became known and gradually replaced Taylorism as the prevailing management belief system and practice.

From Abraham Maslow's 1943 paper: *A Theory of Human Motivation*

Figure 7.1: Maslow's Hierarchy of Needs pyramid

Maslow Changes the Social Contract

Maslow, who founded humanistic psychology, was a professor of psychology at Brandeis University near Boston. In 1943, Maslow published a paper entitled "A Theory of Human Motivation," and in 1954 published his book, *Motivation and Personality*.

Maslow's pyramid, as shown in Figure 7.1, is relatively simple. It states there are five conditions that motivate human beings to act. While most people in business at some time have encountered Maslow's pyramid, let's recap the levels.

Level 1: Physiological or survival needs—food, air, water, shelter

Level 2: Safety needs—a safe place to live, safety of family, safety at work

Level 3: Love—love of family, friends, neighbors and inclusion in social groups

Level 4: Esteem—being well-thought of by those around you

Level 5: Self-actualization—experiencing meaning and realizing inner potential; being self-fulfilled

Maslow's Hierarchy of Needs presupposes that as one level is met, you progress to the next level. However, observation and experience has taught us that people can bounce back and forth between levels. Movement up the pyramid is not stable and can erode over time. For example, people enter Level 5 when they want to feel that they are contributing to the company's mission, but if they do not get paid for a week's work, they move back to Level 2 and no longer care about the mission. Early in people's careers, there may be more interest in esteem and status, but later in careers, retirement security may be a priority.

> In reality, Maslow's levels run parallel, not bottom to top.

Today we recognize that movement between Maslow's levels is parallel. Every day, people need their survival, safety, and belonging needs met or they lack the self-esteem to focus on contributions to the organization and the ability to reach outside of themselves in self-actualizing situations. To understand this phenomenon, ask yourself, "How hard would I work if I felt threatened by job loss on a daily basis?" You might be totally distracted with the ability to perform only the basic requirements of your explicit job description. The more time spent in fear of losing your job, the less time you spend giving discretionary effort.

Because of its negative effect on discretionary effort, fear is clearly not a valuable way for managers to motivate people to get more done. When employees are constantly defenseless against threats, layoffs, and the constant game of politics in the organization, they do not feel psychologically safe. Lack of psychological safety releases cortisol into the blood stream and gives the individual a temporary increase in energy production meant for physical survival.

The fight-or-flight stress response, as discussed in Chapter 5, causes a regular release of cortisol which is harmful to the body as it suppresses the immune system. When employees have cortisol in their system, but they must stand in place at work and behave, then their bodies cannot return to homeostasis by reducing the hormone if they could fight or flee (Wilson n.d.).

Maslow's philosophies greatly affected the social contract in work situations. Figure 7.2 illustrates the changes in interpretation of Maslow's pyramid that have happened as consultants have applied his concepts to the workplace. For employees, physiological needs translate into a paycheck; safety translates into freedom from harassment; love translates into belonging to the team and being part of the work family; esteem translates into recognition for accomplishments at work; and self-actualization is the engagement of the creative abilities of the employee.

Because of Maslow's concepts, managers finally had an outline of what people value in their lives, managers could no longer assume they knew what was best for their employees. Management ultimately became aware of how to *value* employees, and with that, the social contract of the 20th century was born.

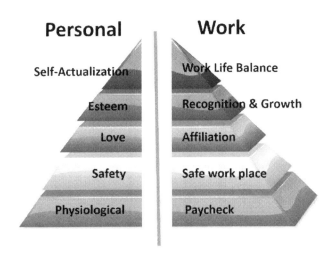

Figure 7.2: How consultants added meaning to Maslow's pyramid

The Practice of Discretionary Effort

Leadership of One Power Principle: Be the leader people choose to follow by leading with positive expectation and refusing to lead with fear.

Reflection

By understanding the social contract of the past and the evolution from Taylorism through Maslow's hierarchy of needs, we can better understand the transition from the *operational-led* value organizational culture to the 21st century *human-led* value culture. The *operational-led* value social contract creates added services and products efficiently and effectively but inhibits discretionary effort because workers do what they are told to do. A *human-led* value social contract cultivates discretionary effort because workers are asked to resolve problems and challenges by using their intellectual powers. An *operational-led* value system is focused on the measurement of what is happening in the moment. A *human-led* value is focused on what can be if employees release discretionary effort. This knowledge helps organizations assess their social contracts and evaluate their workability, or what is working and what is not working. After assessing the existing social contracts, the work starts to introduce new elements that support organizational goals.

The social contract is complex and will keep evolving as we move through the decades. The next chapter introduces ideas for creating updated, 21st century social contracts that release discretionary effort.

Discretionary Effort Exercise:

Drive Out Fear

Fear was an essential component of management in the early 20th century social contract and it still lingers today. Returning to the wisdom of an important management consultant, Edward Deming (2002) asked organizations to cease to motivate with fear because it diminishes energy. We add that as fear diminishes energy, it therefore diminishes discretionary effort. Likewise, Maslow identified a theory of motivation that focused on basic human needs (physiological, safety, love, self-esteem and self-actualization) and their fulfillment. Fear inhibits the process of meeting any of these needs, which is another way that fear obstructs discretionary effort. In short, employees will not give discretionary effort just because they are threatened or it is demanded of them. It is a free-will choice that becomes a gift from the employee to the employer.

Your assignment for this chapter is to recognize and identify fear-based motivations within the social contract operating in your organization. Let the words "Dispel fear" run through your mind. When you are responding to challenges, ask, "Am I operating out of fear? Am I creating fear in my employees by my management approach?" Finally, assess the degree of fear in the organizational culture. Fear is subtle; people will attempt to hide it, deny it, suppress it, or project it on others.

Discretionary Effort Practice Steps

Step 1: Observe and Experience. In the course of your day, be mindful of driving out fear. Use this saying as a reminder to observe fear in yourself and how you react under fear. How productive are you when you are working in the fear mode? Assess what you communicate to others. See if you can perceive fear being used as a motivator in your organization.

Step 2: Contemplate and Record. Maintain a journal or voice recording that chronicles your experiences of observing the amount of fear in the implicit social contract and its impact on the release of discretionary effort.

Step 3: Share, Learn and Model. After you have evaluated the following questions, share your insights and ask for input from a mentor, a friend, or a trusted advisor.

1. What personal breakthroughs did I have when contemplating my levels of fear and observing how I work when operating in the fear mode? If any, what breakdowns related to fear did I have?
2. How is fear expressed in the organization? How is it communicated?

3. What fear-based implicit social contract agreements exist in the organization?
4. How do I plan to drive out fear and release discretionary effort?

References

Deming, W. E. (2002). *Out of the crisis*. Cambridge: Massachusetts Institute of Technology, Center for Advanced Engineering Study.

Maslow, A. H. (1943). A theory of human motivation. *Psychological Review*, 50(4), 370-396. doi:10.1037/h0054346

Maslow, A. H. (1954). *Motivation and personality*. Oxford, England: Harpers.

Taylor, F. W. (2012). *The Principles of scientific management*. Auckland: The Floating Press.

Ulrich, D., & Ulrich, W. (2010). *The why of work: How great leaders build abundant organizations that win.* New York: McGraw-Hill.

Wilson, J. L. (n.d.). Cortisol and adrenal function. *AdrenalFatigue.org*. Retrieved from https://adrenalfatigue.org/cortisol-adrenal-function/

CHAPTER 8

The 21st Century Social Contract

"We had been collecting tons of statistics because they were interesting. But statistics will not construct automobiles—so out they went."
~ Henry Ford, My Life and Work, 1922

The relationship between management and workers has always had a shifting power base of rights, responsibilities, obligations and expectations between employers and employees. When the economy is poor, employers have the upper hand because jobs are scarce and employees hang on for dear life. When the economy improves, employees move into the power position because jobs are plentiful and they can pick and choose the job with the best benefits and social contract.

> The 21st century social contract focuses on shared power, mutual respect, and discretionary effort.

Outdated 20th century management philosophies built on employer power resulted in large gulfs between management and workers. The new social contract of the 21st century differs because it is designed to focus on shared power, mutual respect for talents, and the release of discretionary effort.

The Social Contract and Company Culture

Another word for the social contract is culture. Culture is an immense mass of energy that absorbs and captures individual choices, systems and structures inside the organization. All the mistakes, the gaffes, the blunders as well as the kindnesses, the teamwork, and the successes fill the atmosphere of the organization like a cloud. These innumerable dealings are part of the culture and determine the social contact interactions. When the company hits a tough spell, the culture resembles a storm cloud. When times are good, the cloud can resemble the billowy summer clouds. Culture has consequences that dictate the social contract and impact your return on investment.

> Profitability is a combination of well-being, human dignity, and social acceptance.

One thing is clear: the cloud of culture moves slowly across the atmosphere of the organization and it is difficult to change the direction. The culture changes as employees understand, accept and react to what they believe is valued by leadership.

As clouds of the 21st century social contract and culture drifts through the organization, and employees experience an inevitable storm cloud, employees ask themselves questions that reflect personal concerns. They ask themselves "Am I being benefited by being here? Will I be rewarded for my discretionary effort? Will management listen to my ideas and act upon them?"

The emerging 21st century social contract defines the nature and shape of discretionary effort at the individual and organizational level. At the organizational level, the new social contract recognizes and embraces well-being, human dignity, and social acceptance as cornerstones of profitability. When implemented properly, discretionary effort is released in the form of creative energy. This creative energy regenerates individual enthusiasm and infuses innovative ideas into company products and services which eventually find their way into the marketplace, changing it forever.

> Employees give discretionary effort in the form of increased energy and creative ideas.

When the culture and the implicit social contract is accepted by employees, they give discretionary effort in the form of creative ideas and increased energy. They experience individual growth and daily tasks feel like play, not work. Their personal confidence improves; their total life experience is enriched by complementing their personal and professional lives.

Social Contract Assessments

For increased profitability and economic sustainability in the 21st century, it is important to assess the organization's social contract. This assessment includes an evaluation of the strategic direction and vital processes of the company. The purpose of this assessment is to identify the actions and forces that are suppressing or releasing discretionary effort. Here are important considerations:

1. To discern the relationship between human-led value and the operational-led value, ask:
   a. What are the elements of the explicit and implicit social agreements in our company?
   b. What is the existing balance between human-led value and operational-led value?
   c. What are the driving forces for discretionary effort? What are the inhibitors?
2. To apply the RossBrandau Leadership Model, do the following:
   a. Identify the current relationship between safety, security, and well-being
   b. Identify the relationship between social acceptance and human dignity
   c. Rate employee alignment with your company goals on a scale of 1-10
   d. Rate the emotional engagement of your employees in the company's success on a scale of 1-10
   e. Rate the level of risk-taking permitted in your company

The Assessment and Metrics

The assessment includes rethinking the role of metrics in the organization which can change the way the enterprise operates. If only profitability is measured in a company, quality and safety will be considered secondary, and actions will support that attitude. When workers are told that safety and quality result in profitability, then safety and quality work in tandem to increase profitability. In simple terms, when you change the way the game is scored, you change the game.

> When workers are told that safety and quality result in profitability, all three improve.

For example, a company may want to become the number one supplier of a certain good or service. If the important metric is just-in-time delivery to the customer, quality and waste may not be as important as getting the product in the customer's hands quickly. Accordingly, employees will not worry about increasing costs by stopping the production line to fix a singular problem that affects just-in-time delivery. They may also decide not to fix the problem; instead, they simply may discard the offending part and label it as waste. If metrics were quality or cost, the strategy of throwing out the defective part would count as failure. Another metric is economic value. Economic value is a measure of the benefit provided by a good or service to a customer or employee. The metric is the value in terms of money and is built around the idea, "What is the maximum amount of money a person or organization is willing and able to pay for the good or service?" This is the common standard of measurement in the world today.

Quality of Life Assessments

Profitability may receive more attention, but another kind of measurement that is equally important is assessing the well-being of employees. One such measurement is the Quality of Life (QoL) index developed by Dr. Robert Schalock and colleagues (2002).

Schalock developed the QoL index for the *Handbook on Quality of Life for Human Service Practitioners.* It is an internationally validated framework for measuring the well-being of employees. In attempts to help employees improve their overall health, most companies begin to offer many of the well-being elements Schalock identifies.

Some of these well-being and quality of life offerings include physical fitness facilities, financial assistance, social health services, mentor programs, and team building exercises. If your company offers these benefits, it pays to measure their effects. Treat these benefits like other metrics such as quality, cost, and just-in-time delivery.

A second assessment of well-being is the True Value Metrics (TVM). Peter Burgess (2016) developed TVM to improve the perspective of what needs to be measured. His work documented at truevaluemetrics.org points to the difficulty with using value in metrics because value is subjective and therefore not easy to quantify. Improving employees' quality of life is not about just about increased pay or more time off work. It is about fulfillment of life at work.

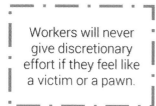

Workers will never give discretionary effort if they feel like a victim or a pawn.

Quality of life is an issue because individuals resist being seen as a victim of management or a pawn as Taylor saw them. Today's 21st century workers want to direct their own lives and to make intelligent choices about their careers. In legal terms, it means employees have agency and permission to make decisions or give input on tasks that affect them. An effective 21st century social contract, therefore, must recognize the agency of employees as a strategy in releasing discretionary effort.

Feedback Sessions

Another way leaders can understand the existing social contract, which comprises the implicit rules employees are following, is to have managers review job descriptions and job expectations in regular feedback sessions. Unlike the annual performance review, feedback sessions are less formal and conducted as needed. The feedback sessions help managers gain valuable insight from the employee's point of view on the challenges and the bumps the company is currently experiencing. During the feedback sessions, managers learn why or why not something is working.

These feedback sessions provide a valuable baseline for understanding the 21st century social contract and make it possible to measure what is not so measurable. Integrity and trust between the manager and the employee is built by seeking and responding to feedback.

For instance, if Jim sold 70 widgets and Pam sold 100, the sales manager would probably assume that Pam gave more effort than Jim, suggesting that unlike Pam, Jim is not pulling his weight. In reality, there are many variables in the sales process: the clients or territories assigned, the extra committees or teams the person is part of, the expertise of the sales person, and so on. Therefore, the feedback session is really a starting place to see how you can help your sales people be more successful. As you help them see a vision of achievement, you are engaging them and moving them to choose to give discretionary effort.

In these feedback sessions, managers can help employees envision the achievements that can be attained through giving discretionary effort. At the same time, feedback sessions reinforce an important part of the new social contract: the organization will notice and reward employees' discretionary effort.

Surfacing the Truth in the 21st Century Culture

Another way to understand and forge the new 21st century culture is to permit employees to surface the truth rather than feed a negative grapevine. One way to do this is called the "as-heard-by" strategy. Doug learned this strategy when working with a senior leadership team.

After interviewing the leaders, Doug brought the senior team together. The president's comments were anonymously included in the as-heard-by document. The document contained different leaders' exact words about issues, challenges, problems and future directions; however, no one knew who said what. At the meeting, the leadership team read the report quickly. Doug had asked the president to be silent and let the team decide themselves on what needed to be done. One director spoke up and the rest followed. The report, they agreed, contained all the unspoken and spoken issues that the team had to deal with. Everything was on the table. The truth had been surfaced. The reality of their situation demanded a response. No one needed to wait for the president to name the solution, for the path forward was clear.

Within 16 months, the organization had increased profitability by 35%. The president never had to say a word except to agree to do his part. The senior team had released their discretionary effort by simply revealing the truth and doing what needed to be done. The same process applies to all teams and departments. Surfacing the truth in an anonymous and no-blame environment is the first step in bringing problems out of the clouds and into the sunlight. It is an organic process of going to the employees and asking them how the problem can be fixed. Once the problem is surfaced, the discretionary effort of every team member is focused on solutions. The culture of discretionary effort will begin to take hold. The solutions will have a multiplier effect throughout the entire organization. As leaders and employees recognize the power of discretionary effort in resolving organizational issues, the social contract will evolve.

> Surfacing the truth creates a solutions-focused team that deals with problems in a straight-forward manner.

Six Steps to Create a 21st Century Social Contract

It may not be obvious, but the social contract in the organization sets the standard for the work ethic of employees. The challenge for every leader is to discern exactly what the current implicit, subconscious social contract is. Like a cloud, the social contract is real but intangible. Workers don't consciously think about the social contract or try to define it. They just do their job in the context with the culture they are experiencing.

The social contract is reshaped as leaders observe the implicit social contract at work in their enterprise and determine what is helping and what is at cross-purposes in achieving the company goals.

> The 21st century social contract redefines workplace excellence.

The following six steps will help you define and change the social contract in your organization. While the steps are straight forward and easy to implement, changing the social contract will take patience and time.

Step 1: Describe the current reality

First, by yourself, sit down and write out on one page what you think and feel is going on with the people of the organization. Because this is a process, don't worry about being right or wrong or whether your observations are complete. It takes time to write down your thoughts and then refine them into a one-page description you can share with others.

Below are questions you can ask yourself as you identify the components of the social contract that specify organizational culture:

1. **Customs**. Can you identify the traditional ways of doing things that are unique to your culture? What are the unwritten rules for doing business in your company?
2. **Attitudes**. Reflect on the mental and emotional states of workers at all levels of the organization. Are they positive or negative?
3. **Behaviors**. Assess the outward manifestations of attitudes by observing the state of team work and interpersonal relationships. Are interactions collaborative and cooperative?
4. **Beliefs**. Do employees know that safety rules are important to follow? Do they firmly believe that others in the organization are watching out for

them? Do they believe your company will identify the distractions and obstacles that hinder performance and economic stability? Do they believe your products and services make a difference in the lives of customers or consumers?

5. **Well-being**. Do individuals care about each other on a personal level? Are managers keyed into the problems employees might be experiencing in their personal lives?

6. **Acceptance**. Are employees accepted "as is" and allowed to grow professionally? Are ethnic groups welcome in your company? Are your managers adept at using the strengths of each individual?

7. **Individual Rights**. As the millennials become an increasingly significant force in the workplace, the social contract is naturally evolving to reflect their passion for individual rights. Today's millennial workers want to have a say in the decisions that affect them and want the authority to execute when given an assignment. They often want the right to telecommute and have more balance in their life-style.

8. **Mentorship**. Are people in the organization willing to mentor less experienced individuals and help them understand and clarify operational processes and systems?

9. **Rumor Mill**. Are issues addressed upfront and not permitted to become part of an underground negative grapevine?

Step 2: Analyze

Once you have observed and described the current situation, then you can analyze the information. You will examine the data you have collected in order to explain it and interpret it. Slowly as you do this, the implicit social contract will emerge right before your eyes. We cannot tell you exactly what you will see, but the implicit social contract will take form in your mind and on paper. Keep it to one page for now. Every organization is different and unique therefore your implicit social contract is not universal. It exists only within your organization.

> The 21st century social contract identifies distractions and obstacles to performance and economic sustainability.

As you analyze, you might identify that the attitudes of people in the organization are generally happy or unhappy. They may be enthusiastic in their work or they may be treating it as an obligation. They may be on time for bosses' meetings but not on time for peer meetings. Respect may be extended to managers above the workers on the organizational chart but not to the workers below.

What do you observe that is happening in the moment and what does it mean to you? You may discover that some of the traditional behaviors don't make sense or that the wrong people are in the wrong meetings. It may be an unwritten rule to avoid conflict at all costs. You may see that some situations keep repeating when they should disappear or that leaders are making decisions with flawed data. Whatever you analyze that is unique to your company, remember that the social contract is a force that if understood can be used to your benefit.

Step 3: Involve others

The next step is to introduce the process to someone close to you. Explain to your mentor what you did, why you did it, and that you are hoping to define the implicit social contract or culture in the organization. Ask for input and observations in a brief written summary. Have a conversation with your mentor, perhaps over lunch, and see if your observations are similar.

There is no right or wrong, there is only discovery of what is helping and what is hurting the organization. As you involve others (choose as many as you like), certain aspects will be validated. When you are satisfied with the collected information, prepare a simple presentation, and ask for input and corroboration by a trusted team.

Step 4: Identify the emerging elements of a new culture

The implicit social contract is manifested in the workers' opinions, and as you involve others and attempt to label and analyze it, the desired living, breathing, new culture will emerge. As the truth surfaces, you can start the work of correcting the direction of your organization's implicit social contract.

Because the idea of an implicit social contract is often difficult to understand, you might define it as the new culture you want to create. Start by identifying the attitudes, the customs, and the behaviors you would like to see in the organization. The description will not be perfect, but you have a starting point. You know where you have been, and you know where you are going. You have input from people you trust that validates and confirms the existing and the desired future state.

In context of discretionary effort leadership, you may want to improve your culture by demonstrating for workers how to acknowledge the effort of others and to have honest discussions about disagreements. Other ways to improve your culture are encouraging employees to surface the truth, giving more mindshare and creative thought to solutions, or exhibiting a more positive attitude when faced with seemingly insurmountable challenges.

Step 5: Model and live the 21st century contract

Resist the urge to start a program or institute a new way of doing things with the assumption that your new program will solve the problems. There is a subtle and more effective way to effect change. You start by changing your own behaviors and adopting the desired changes into your personal leadership style. If you do not live and model the behaviors, they will never become part of your culture.

For example, one powerful way to change the social contract is going from a culture of demanding extra effort from employees to an attitude of gratitude by recognizing employees who give discretionary effort. Another change is moving from a culture of top-down management to involvement of all team members assigned to a project. As workers become more involved, they feel the increased self-worth that comes from contributing. The usual result is a more pleasant work environment.

In one company, Doug saw the two senior leaders spend six months living the newly conceived discretionary effort contract. They learned it by practicing the new culture they wanted in their company. As they observed each other and gave each other feedback, they corrected their attitudes and behaviors to fit the desired new culture.

By the time they held a meeting with their direct reports to discuss their desired new social contract and discretionary effort culture, every member of their staff knew exactly what they were talking about because they had seen it in the way these two astute leaders behaved. You may be interested to know that these two leaders never put forth an action plan in their presentation. They simply asked their senior managers to live the discretionary effort culture necessary to change the implicit social contract in their organization.

Step 6: Trust the process

The process is very natural and in due time a new implicit social contract will take shape and substance, and a new culture of discretionary effort will be established. There may be explicit policies and procedures that result, but more importantly when the senior team lives it and models it, the employees will see, they will follow, and they will adopt the new social contract.

The Practice of Discretionary Effort

LEADERSHIP OF ONE
POWERFUL PRINCIPLE

Leadership of One Power Principle: Be the leader people choose to follow by surfacing the truth as a beginning point in transformation.

Reflection

The implicit social contract of the 21st century is constantly evolving. The direction is toward a culture that values employees and places employees in jobs where they can use their strengths. As they use their strengths, their feelings of self-esteem and self-confidence increase along with their discretionary effort. Increased discretionary effort from employees will move the company forward to crucial economic sustainability.

By noticing and rewarding employee discretionary effort, organizations influence the changing nature of the social contract away from issues that divide the organization to those common values that unite the organization. The organization benefits from a human-led value culture where individual fulfillment and high organizational performance are intertwined. The key to a human-led value culture where high performance flourishes is exposing the truth about the implicit social contract and troublesome processes.

Discretionary Effort Exercise:

Surface the Truth

Surfacing the truth requires strategies and skills from both individuals and organizations. In modern manufacturing organizations, recognizing the truth is critical to identifying and resolving systemic problems that limit organizational profitability. In personal development literature, recognizing and acknowledging the truth about your personal motivations and actions is vital to character and leadership development.

While exposing the truth is deemed difficult by many, the difficulty is born from the belief that individuals can't accept the truth about themselves and/or will be hurt once the truth is out. This may be the prevailing paradigm about telling the truth, but it fails to recognize the benefits of embracing the truth. Done correctly, surfacing the truth is helpful and freeing. In a human-led value culture, bringing the truth to the surface is an event where ignorance, denial and blame are driven out. Revealing the truth allows the organization and people to see a new reality and begin to transform the organization.

The goal of this assignment is to surface the truth about what is happening in your organization. As you go about your daily activities, repeat this phase in your mind: "Surface the truth wherever you see it." Observe both the implicit and explicit aspects of the social contract. Reflect on whether the work being done is operational-led or human-led. As you observe through the lens of truth, it will become clear what you can control, what you can influence, what you need to let go of, and how the social contract is changing.

Saying "Surface the truth" repeatedly inside of your mind frees yourself and others of blame, denial, and ignorance. When this happens, people are free to release their discretionary effort to resolve systemic issues and deal with daily challenges.

Discretionary Effort Practice Steps

Step 1: Observe and Experience. In the course of your day, remind yourself to "surface the truth." Learn to accept the truth as a liberating force. Work to uncover the truth in others in a way that is helpful and kind.

Step 2: Contemplate and Record. Maintain a record of your experiences of surfacing the truth.

Step 3: Share, Learn and Model. After you have evaluated the following questions, share your insights and ask for input from a mentor, a friend, or a trusted advisor.

1. What personal breakthroughs did I have when I practiced surfacing the truth? Did I have any

breakdowns or have trouble facing the truth about myself as it surfaced?

2. What organizational breakthroughs did I have as I worked to let others identify the truth? What breakdowns did I observe about the organizational ability to uncover the truth when dealing with problems and issues?

3. What is the relationship between surfacing the truth and discretionary effort?

4. How will I model surfacing the truth within my organization?

References

Burgess, P. (2016, March 19). What is true value accounting? The framework needed for better metrics. *True Value Metrics*. Retrieved from http://www.slideshare.net/PeterBurgess2/tva-for-mdm-1of10

Schalock, R. L., & Alonso, M. V. (2002). *Handbook on quality of life for human service practitioners.* Washington, DC: American Association on Mental Retardation.

CHAPTER 9

Leadership Level 3: Rational Alignment

"The energy of each individual cell in the corporate body must be actively recruited. This requires aligning individual and organizational purpose. Alignment drives performance. Lack of alignment significantly restricts the quantity, quality, direction and focus of available energy."
~ *Jim Loehr and Tony Schwartz, The Power of Full Engagement*

Figure 9.1: Leadership Level 3, Rational Alignment

The third level of the RossBrandau Leadership Model, Rational Alignment, illustrated in Figure 9.1, can be defined as providing the leadership umbrella of mission, values, vision, goals, objectives and strategy so employees can rationally align with the organization.

Alignment is a word used in many professions. In the chiropractic world, the spine must be aligned for optimal health. In the automotive industry, tires must be aligned according to the manufacturer's specifications. When a car's tires individually point too far in or too far out, they work against each other promoting premature tire wear and increasing fuel usage. In physics, the alignment of electrons is what makes material magnetic. If half of the electrons spin one way and the rest spin the other way, they will neutralize each other and the material will never be a magnet.

> Workers need to be aligned like electrons in a magnet.

When employees in different units in the organization are spinning in opposite directions or pointing in different directions, they are working against each other and are not aligning. Aligned employees become magnets that attract customers, build the brand, and improve marketplace positioning. As stated so well in the quote at the beginning of the chapter by Jim Loehr and Tony Schwartz (2003), alignment is critical to the success of the company as it not only turns employees into magnets but it drives productivity and increases value creation.

Value creation is increasing the worth of goods and services with the end goal of increasing profits. This is the primary aim of any business entity and many experts recommend value creation as the primary goal and first priority of all employees. It is the ability to create value for customers that sells products and services, and at the same time, creates value for shareholders, increases stock prices, and insures an economically sustainable future.

Ken Favaro (1998) explains in *Put Value Creation First*, "If you put value creation first in the right way, your managers will know where and how to grow the business; they will deploy capital better than your competitors; and they will develop more talent than your competition. This will give you an enormous advantage in building your company's ability to achieve profitable and long-lasting growth." Rational thought gives workers the ability to intellectually relate to and the opportunity to align with company policies.

In order to be rationally aligned, there must be an underlying logic for everything that is done in an organization. It is characterized by a systematic approach to execute the future created by the vision, mission, and goals generated by the founder(s) and the leadership team. When an organization is rationally aligned, the approach to answering organizational questions is based on reason and rational choice.

> Rational means workers can intellectually relate to and align with company policies.

Reason is the capacity for consciously making sense of what is currently happening in the organization, applying logic, establishing and verifying facts, and changing or justifying practices, processes, and beliefs based on new or existing information. Thinking uses reason to move from one idea to a related idea. For example, reason draws the alignment between cause and effect, truth or lies. The concept of reason is sometimes referred to as rationality. Rationality is the process of reasoning that improves decision-making and evaluations based on cost-versus-benefit, pain versus gain, and develops strategies to maximize advantages or minimize disadvantages.

Figure 9.2 Relationship between rational alignment and organizational success

Rational Alignment and Organizational Success

With the definitions for the words *rational* and *alignment* in mind, it is important to look at how these ideas work together to drive organizational success. Rational alignment is built up of elements found in the mission, values, vision, goals and strategy developed by the leadership team. In Figure 9.2, notice that at this point, the flow is from top to bottom.

Once the leadership team communicates this information to the managers, the managers are free to develop their own departmental goals and project plans. The purpose of developing their own personal departmental goals and project plans is to use their creativity, knowledge and intellect in determining how the company strategy will be implemented. They have the obligation to write goals and objectives that are ambitious and aggressive with specific metrics and deadlines that will move employees into action.

When the goals and objectives are well written, it is each manager's responsibility to invite individual employees to rationally and intellectually align with them. It is the individual employee's opportunity to accept the invitation and their responsibility to ask the following questions:

"Do my values align with the company values?"

"Can I support the company mission?"

"Can I see the same vision my leaders see?"

"Do I have the expertise to contribute to the goals of the company?"

"Can I find satisfaction and self-fulfillment in what I do here?"

When employees answer these questions in the affirmative and accept the invitation to rationally align with the organization, they are in a position to give discretionary effort and contribute to the overall value creation of the department. Their commitment and loyalty to the organization increases and they are in a position to point their daily productivity toward company goals. Now the process is bottom to top.

> Rational alignment is a commonsense framework for releasing discretionary effort in workers.

Rational alignment is taken for granted by upper management and leaders are often surprised and confused when employees are foggy about the purpose and goals of the company. For instance, Doug worked with a manager in a very busy organization. In a tour of the floor, he and the manager came across an employee sitting at a rest station doing nothing. The manager was completely comfortable with the employee's lack of activity. It turns out that the employee was a maintenance mechanic, and if he was doing nothing, then everything in the department was working properly. The employee explained, "They only need me when things are not going well."

Although perfectly rational to the employee and the manager, it made no sense to Doug. He inquired about preventive maintenance practices for all the machines. The manager explained that they did regular maintenance according to the manufacturer's specifications but had no predictive or standardized maintenance procedures. When machines broke, they were fixed.

Doug asked again how often the machines went down and what the impact was. The manager explained that machine downtime was the biggest barrier to success. He explained that was why the manager kept this employee ready to go at a moment's notice. Doug inquired again how many machines the employee was responsible for and the answer was all of them. Naturally, the next inquiry was, "How often are one or more machines down at the same time?" The manager was not sure but explained machines being down at the same time happened on a regular basis. In fact, the manager was thinking of getting another maintenance mechanic to resolve that problem.

Doug then asked how much of the employee's time was spent fixing broken machinery. The manager did not know. Sometimes the employee would go a week without work and other times he would have to work overtime and weekends to get the machinery going. Doug wondered why such a critical part of production was so problematic and wondered what would happen to the machinery if this employee suddenly left the job.

The lack of predictive maintenance and the over-reliance on this person were illogical when the manager's goal should have been to decrease downtime due to repairs. Decreased downtime would permit the department to stay on track to reach company production goals. The employee was only rationally aligned and integrated into the value creation process on an "as needed" basis. Clarifying the goals and strategy of the company in the mind of this manager and the employee would drastically improve production.

Three Steps to Information Alignment

Rationally aligned employees are at the core of a human-led value culture. When leadership knows that the employees have the information they need to make the right decisions and make them in real time, it can let go of top-down management.

There are three important steps leaders can take to engage employees and encourage them to align and enable them to give discretionary effort: communicating, informing, and motivating.

> A leader improves productivity by providing clarity on the goals, strategy, and direction of the company.

Step 1: Communicating Clearly

Would you get on a jet if you discovered the pilot had no flight plan, didn't really know where he was going, and had no idea how much gas he had in his tank? No, of course not. By providing clear messages for your organization, you are in effect giving everyone a flight plan. A clear flight plan moves people out of their comfort zones, establishes direction for a specific period of time, identifies expected results, and sets targets. Clear goals and objectives enable employees to know when they have successfully completed their tasks.

In an effort to define their values, mission and vision, many leadership teams spend hours in deliberation, go on training retreats, or even invite consultants to examine every detail of the company. All that time and effort is in vain if the teams then permit ambiguity in their goals and objectives and cause a foggy direction for employees. Because goals and objectives are key ingredients of efficient performance, the directives need to be written in plain English: avoid esoteric jargon and cleverly crafted acronyms. When goals and objectives are well-written, business units and teams know exactly what is expected of them.

Specific and deadline-based goals and objectives become a strategy for employee productivity. A strategy by definition is a starting point. It sets the chosen direction and describes the principal initiatives and projects necessary to achieve the company goals and mission. Business schools, management gurus and consultants regularly develop new approaches and methodologies for strategy formulation and all acknowledge its overwhelming importance in setting the tone for the organization and its prospects for success. Simply put, strategy links the mission and goals to current reality. Strategy applies to all employees in the company and should focus them on the path forward.

In today's world, we could use a hypothetical example of the new tech company intent on dominating the sales software market; in fact, they had a mission to completely command the direction of the entire market. The start-up software company needs to choose which type of company will be their target; their options range from a complex, multi-level sales firm to a one-man sales effort. The start-up company has choices to make. If the company decides to direct its software for larger sales companies, that choice dictates the strategy for the entire workforce. The decision affects the word choice in marketing brochures and the website; it defines the avenues for sales leads. The entire workforce concentrates and aligns with marketing to the right buyer.

Simply said, a strategy is a choice between two or more alternatives. Once the leadership team has clarified the choice and direction, employees can concentrate their efforts. Concentration of effort can be achieved with a formal goal deployment or by providing a system of key performance indicators with built-in follow up.

However, in one plant where we consulted, the strategy adoption was done quite informally. The plant manager announced that he wanted every department to come up with one way to reduce waste and increase efficiency in their area. He set a goal of a $600,000 in savings in one month. One requirement was to follow proper protocol in involving engineering and quality control before implementing any change in the system. The changes were to be simple and implementable with sustainable results. The organization met and exceeded that goal by almost 30 percent without a hiccup in production or quality.

Simply put, strategy links the mission and goals to current reality and gives the company leverage to compete in the worldwide marketplace, as illustrated in Figure 9.3.

Step 2: Informing

With clear directives in hand, the challenging task begins of informing and aligning all employees. Despite its significance, aligning an organization remains one of the most elusive and unsatisfactory areas of management. Perhaps because the leadership team feels that after articulating the mission, goals, and strategy, then it is redundant to keep repeating it. A false assumption is made: if employees hear the message at the company-wide meeting, then they automatically internalize it and act on it. Indeed, repetition is exactly what is needed to make the corporate message and roadmap a true motivator for employees.

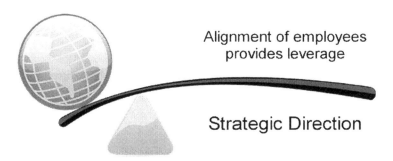

Figure 9.3: Alignment working with strategic direction

In *The Strategy-Focused Organization: How Balanced Scorecard Companies Thrive in the New Business Environment*, Robert S. Kaplan and David P. Norton (2000) state that only 21 percent of middle managers and a mere seven percent of employees have their personal goals aligned to those of their company.

This fact explains why there may be a ton of visual activity at a company—people look busy—but not a lot of bottom-line results. When people's work is not aligned and focused on the company's business goals, their lack of focus reduces competitiveness and profitability. Improved focus makes your company smarter and more cohesive than your competitors, giving you a competitive advantage with accompanying increased financial performance.

According to Kaplan and Norton, "Less than five percent of the typical workforce understands their organization's strategy." These are strategies that the leadership team thinks are engrained into the fabric of their employees' every day work life.

Bringing a sense of reality to this research, Harvard Business School professor John P. Kotter (2011) wrote an article entitled, "Think You're Communicating Enough? Think Again." In this article, Kotter said, "Most companies under communicate their visions for change by at least a factor of ten. A single memo announcing a big new change is never enough, nor is even a series of speeches by the CEO and the executive team." His rationale for this statement is based on the extraordinary number of communications that bombard employees on a monthly basis. Typically, a change in vision receives an inadequate introduction with a "30-minutes speech, one hour-long meeting, or a 600-word article" which translates into .0058 percent of the communications an employee processes within a 3-month period (Kotter 2011).

The messages that motivate employees to align must be repeated in company memos, emails, large group meetings, small group meetings, posters in the hallways, and in informal conversations. Make the messages visible in the lunchroom, mentioned in one-on-one discussions by the manager with the employee, and written in the company newsletter. To capture attention, make the statements simple but rich in language. Express ideas in metaphors, analogies, examples, and stories.

Most important, use your skills of personal leadership, the leadership of one. The more you as a leader demonstrate the vision, mission, strategy, and goals of the organization, the more easily employees will align, knowing what the direction of the organization looks like and what it means in practical application.

When the employees walking down the hall include the strategy and goals in their casual conversations, you know you have communicated the message so many times that everyone understands it.

Step 3: Motivating from the Bottom-Up

After creating clear messages and informing employees, the third stage of alignment is getting workers to embrace company goals as their own. Most employees want to have a measurable impact on the business but don't know how to do so. As the research shows, because of lack of communication, employees are not clued into corporate objectives and strategies. They don't always see the correlation between their own personal work and the company goals because they don't understand the organization's priorities.

Once your leadership team has created the *where we are going* and *why we are going*, it is time to turn the *how* over to the managers of business units and to the project teams. The managers and supervisors can now work in collaboration with employees to establish the individual employee's role in the company's success. This process establishes the correlation between their work tasks and company success.

> Employees need to be able to understand the organization priorities and their role in contributing to success.

Employees who understand how they contribute to the overall company mission and how the company objectives are relevant to them are more motivated workers. The key to sustained motivation is to show them how they can achieve more in the company if their individual goals are aligned with corporate goals.

This motivational part of the alignment process moves the company mission and goals from the abstract to specific goals that a department, business unit, or team can write in precise and measurable terms complete with a deadline. The more an organization includes and engages its employees in this process, the greater pride the workers feel in the work produced. They have the power of focus which keeps them from being caught up in the B- and C-level tasks talked about in time management circles and gives them the discipline to work on the critical A-level tasks. The workers give their A-tasks discretionary effort and the company achieves superior business results.

Managerial attention is a critical component for maintaining motivation and alignment. It is important that the manager works with the employee to set crystal clear individual goals and objectives that meet the department's strategy and objectives. Employees are more motivated when they have permission to use their individual initiative in choosing *how I will get there* rather than being told blindly *do this* and then *do that*.

Using their individual initiative permits them to draw their own roadmap for achievement. Regular accountability sessions with each employee ensure the worker's roadmap is leading to on-time completion of projects. As opposed to micromanaging official visits, supportive check points with employees could be as informal as a stop at their office or cubical to say something like, "How's the project progressing? Are there any barriers to completion I need to be aware of?" Perhaps a simple text is appropriate: "R U still on target?"

Throughout the process of goal alignment and managerial attention, employee contributions will not peak and then drop but will continue to climb, keeping the organization competitive. Often employees who are thoroughly aligned and motivated in turn stimulate a leadership team to increase their management support. For example, a motivated management team would ensure needed resources and training is provided, negotiate timelines, break down barriers, and routinely ask what blocks to action are prohibiting completion of the project. When employees influence their leadership you have what is called *motivation from the bottom-up*.

Five Keys to Increasing Organizational Alignment

When employees align with the organizational mission and goals, all aspects of the organization can operate as one entity. Here are the five key aspects within an organization that leaders can look at to determine alignment strengths and weaknesses.

1. Positioning: Employees need to be positioned for success by giving them the tools, resources, people (appropriate team members), and information they need to do their job. An employee's ability to rationally align is disrupted when there is disconnect between what performance is expected and what support is provided.

2. Integration: Different people, structures, processes, objectives, documents, and transactions are independent and interdependent. The challenge is to integrate and align rationally so that all aspects of an organization operate efficiently and effectively as one whole.

3. Standardization: Conforming to a replicable procedure, process, or technical standard results in a consistent, efficient outcome. An antonym for standardization is customization. Standardization of elements of the organizational complexity allows for simplicity and clarity to combat chaos and confusion.

4. Coordination: Coordination is a managerial function of adjusting and interlinking different activities of the business, resolving disagreements, and continually evaluating suggestions and recommendations for changes. Coordination provides guidance and clarity among individuals so they work cooperatively to achieve the desired goals.

5. Continuous Improvement: Once people are rationally aligned, anything that isn't working will become obvious. Employees who are focused on continuous improvement will fix those problems.

Employees who are rationally aligned and motivated are at the core of a human-led value culture. They work more efficiently and creatively toward their individual goals which have been set to align with departmental goals and company goals. Alignment makes the employees an organization's competitive advantage.

The Practice of Discretionary Effort

LEADERSHIP OF ONE POWERFUL PRINCIPLE

Leadership of one Power Principle: To be the leader people choose to follow, align with company goals to replace chaos with order.

Reflection

Harry Lauder said, "The future is not a gift—it is an achievement." Let's add: a future of achievement made possible by the miracle of alignment.

In order to embrace a human-led value culture, leadership needs to know that employees are acting in alignment with the organization. Aligning the organization by the principles in this chapter creates a shared sense of a bright and successful future. The vision motivates and coordinates the kinds of actions among employees that create innovation and transformation at every level. It is one thing to be rationally aligned, but to execute plans, employees must also be emotionally committed. They need to know that what they do matters.

Discretionary Effort Exercise:

Replace Chaos with Order

Rational alignment replaces disorder and misalignment with order. Chaos reigns in an organization without direction. As the vision, values, mission and company direction and goals are discussed and implemented, they help employees rationally align and know where to channel their energy. Encourage all employees to align with the company direction and to have integrity by doing the right thing (see Chapter 2), and order will emerge out of chaos. Helping employees make their way through chaos to order is relevant and worthy of your best efforts. Order cannot be imposed, but like putting a jigsaw puzzle together, as your team finds the right pieces, order is created.

Discretionary Effort Practice Steps

Step 1: Observe and Experience. In the course of your day, identify where confusion and chaos is happening. Can you help restore order? What kind of chaos are you experiencing inside? Can you calm the disruptions inside?

 Step 2: Contemplate and Record. Maintain a record of your experiences of finding the chaos in ordinary situations and how you worked to resolve the chaos. Was focusing the goals of the company and aligning employees with them helpful? Did revisiting the goals provide direction?

 Step 3: Share, Learn and Model. After you have evaluated the following questions, share your insights and ask for input from a mentor, a friend or trusted advisor.

1. What personal breakthroughs did I have in observing chaos and turning it around by remembering the direction of the company? What breakdowns did I have and how did I resolve the disruption?
2. What organizational breakdowns on teams did I observe? Did I see breakthroughs as people encountered confusion and chaos and realigned with the goals of the company?
3. What is the relationship between finding order in chaos and releasing discretionary effort?
4. What is my strategy to model replacing chaos with order in the environment?

References

Favaro, K. (1998). Put value creation first: If you want to grow your way to greatness. *Marakon Commentary*. Retrieved from http://www.favaro.net/publications/pvcf/ken_pvcf.html

Kaplan, R. S., & Norton, D. P. (2001). *The strategy-focused organization: How balanced scorecard companies thrive in the new business environment*. Boston: Harvard Business Review Press.

Kotter, J. P. (2011, June 14). Think you're communicating enough? Think again. *www.forbes.com*. Retrieved from http://www.forbes.com/sites/johnkotter/2011/06/14/think-youre-communicating-enough-think-again

Loehr, J. E., & Schwartz, T. (2003). *The power of full engagement: Managing energy, not time, is the key to high performance and personal renewal*. New York: Free Press.

CHAPTER 10

Leadership Level 4:
Emotional Commitment

"Highly committed employees perform up to 20 percentile points better than less committed employees, and are 87 percent less likely to leave the organization than employees with low levels of commitment."
~ *Study by North Carolina State Office of Personnel*

RossBrandau Discretionary Effort Leadership Model

PROFITABILITY AND ECONOMIC SUSTAINABILITY

Authentic Contribution

Emotional Commitment

Rational Alignment

Social Acceptance

Safety and Security

WORK ENVIRONMENT OF INTEGRITY AND GRATITUDE

Figure 10.1: Leadership Level 4, Emotional Commitment

Leadership Level 4 deals with a mysterious quality called emotional commitment. The goal is to lead employees through the steps from being a worker who just works for a paycheck to one that emotionally commits to the organization and gives discretionary effort. To help the employee reach the goal, a leader has the responsibility to personally commit to the growth and well-being of each direct report. It also requires leadership transparency.

Doug learned about transparency in an interesting way. The senior officer of a company, we'll call him Sean, invited Doug to a decision making session he was conducting with his managers for the specs on a new product due out in six months. Sean boldly announced that Doug would be pleasantly surprised at his prowess in conducting this session and the results he would achieve.

He started the session by briefly laying out three options then announcing emphatically that he preferred Option 1. Sean then asked for their opinions. One hour later, the group decided Option 1 was not a good option and gingerly tiptoed around Sean to discuss Options 2 and 3. Two hours later, the group suggested Option 2 was the best choice.

Sean bowed his head and appeared to be in deep thought. After a minute or two he raised his head, smiled and said, "You convinced me. We'll implement Option 2." As the managers left the room, they felt that something was not quite right about the three hours they had just spent in their meeting with Sean. Their gut feelings were right. The grapevine in the company later revealed that Sean and the president of the company had already decided on Option 2. His statement that he preferred Option 1, which was an obviously horrible option, was a ploy to get the managers involved in conversation and make them think they were engaged in the process, that their opinions counted, and that they were contributing to the growth of the company.

Emotional commitment requires leadership transparency.

What Sean actually did was demonstrate a lack of leadership transparency. He wasted three hours of ten top managers' time (and an estimated five thousand dollars of company money when you compute the hourly rate of each manager) while eroding the priceless commodity of trust the managers could place in him. Sean could say he engaged his managers in the decision, but emotional commitment to a product and its success was lacking because integrity was not in Sean's actions. Sean was phony and his interactions with the employees were a façade. Management was playing the game of being transparent.

Unfortunately for the senior leaders, their ploy was obvious, so they were being much more transparent than they knew, and the managers were not fooled.

The lesson here is that those in leadership are often transparent even when they think they are not. It is puzzling that leaders think they are smarter than their employees and that they can hide their emotions and real intentions. Incidentally, when this company's stocks went from twenty-four dollars to 3, Sean and senior management blamed the economy, rather than admitting their leadership deficiencies. Leaders need to be genuine, authentic and trustworthy if they want to receive their employees' commitment and authenticity in return. Some of the most common mistakes managers make is believing they are gaining emotional commitment, when instead they are just engaging employees.

Emotionally Committed or Just Engaged?

Some leadership teams think engagement and emotional commitment are synonymous. They are not. The term engagement is a 20th century term which involves the carrot and stick approach: benefits, bonuses, incentive catalogs, subsidized lunchrooms, retirement and health benefits. These carrots, which may not be sustainable in the 21st century economy, are all external attempts to yield enthusiastic, hard-working employees.

Popular engagement strategies encourage managers to run contests, administer countless employee engagement surveys, or offer meritless awards. These engagement tactics often have the opposite effect: employees who feel like victims, have less incentive to work, and engage in unfriendly competition. Some of these programs distract employees from actual work. Any good manager will continue the actions that do engage the worker but will stop massive engagement programs that add to the cost of the product and become entitlements, not rewards.

Unless your employees are highly engaged and emotionally committed to the mission of your organization, they will expend the level of effort required to stay in your organization, but not move your organization forward. Consider the following four examples.

First there is an employee named Pat. Pat is highly engaged with passion and enthusiasm because she likes the easy job she landed and can hardly believe her good luck. She has good skills and can complete her assigned tasks effortlessly even though she doesn't necessarily like or feel emotionally attached to the company. She stays because the job doesn't overtax her energy.

Then there is Rolf. Rolf appears to be highly engaged because he loves what he *receives* from the organization. He likes the "free" deluxe meal in the lunch room on Fridays and the convenient social network of coworkers who go out to the bar with him after work. Still, Rolf doesn't necessarily have high output. When given heavy assignments, his engagement takes a noticeable dive.

Next there is Tim. Tim has a high level of engagement because he loves what the job will do for his career, but he is not necessarily loyal to the company. He is proactive because he is motivated to develop his own *skill sets* and he, too, can be emotionally detached from the company. Tim stays long enough to catapult himself into a better position—whether it be at your company or another company, he does not care. If the next headhunter calls with even a little bump in pay, he will be out the door, taking your intellectual property with him.

Finally, there is Nicole. She can be observed as having a high level of engagement because she is on a quest to *save the organization* even though she probably does not hold the organization in high esteem. She is proactive because it feeds her ego that with her great abilities, she can spot problems and fix them. She is emotionally detached from the company and stays because she believes they would collapse without her knowledge and intelligence. Her demeanor is often cool, and she never sincerely opens up in a genuine or authentic fashion. The grapevine says she looks down her nose at people in inferior positions.

These are personal, social, or selfish individual reasons for being engaged. When leaders can move employees past these personal reasons for engagement, the employees begin to align with the organization as described in Chapter 9, Rational Alignment, setting the stage for discretionary effort. Employees slowly transition from giving the minimum acceptable level of work for a paycheck to being engaged with the maximum level of energy and output. As their personal goals run parallel to company purposes, employees and the company both win.

Here are three behaviors managers take part in that reduce the emotional commitment of employees:

1. **Lack of Follow Through.** To gauge the difference between engagement and emotional commitment in your organization, imagine you are an employee sitting in a planning meeting and engaged in a conversation about company strategies. Your mind is generating ideas for implementation, but at the end of the meeting there are no assignments. After the meeting there is no follow-up. You would be hard pressed to write goals and create daily task lists that support company strategies.

2. **One-way Communication.** Like most managers, you may think you are extremely effective at engaging employees in personal conversations that start with rapport-building, superficial chitchat before outlining the assignment for the next few weeks. You may walk away thinking the employee gladly accepted the project, remembering he responded well during their rapport-building conversation. If, however, the employee asked no pertinent questions about how to carry out the assignment nor asked for any clarifications, you may have engaged in one-way communication: giving your thoughts to the employee. The employee gave you no honest feedback in return and may not have emotionally committed to the project.

3. **Short-Term Rewards.** Another familiar engagement example is the annual awards banquet. You host a glamorous event. All

employees arrive wearing their finest clothes. They enjoy the lavish meal and watch as you hand out awards to those considered the top ten employees. What you don't see is how the other employees feel left out, and how they also deserved recognition for their efforts. Even though they appear engaged in the event, eating the five-course dinner, laughing at the jokes, and clapping for the award recipients, they may leave the event with decreased incentive to be emotionally committed.

Do these descriptions leave anything out? Have you experienced similar happenings? As a leadership team, evaluate these supposed engagement activity examples. While these types of activities may have their place, are they earning you the results you want, or are they failing to help employees gain emotional commitment?

In the context of organizations, emotional commitment can be described as the extent to which employees have attachment and loyalty to the organization and are excited, even passionate or zealous about their work. Leadership Level 4, Emotional Commitment, shown in Figure 10.1, gives managers the understanding and tools they need to gain and retain the emotional commitment of their employees.

The Stages of Emotional Commitment

Emotional commitment is a raw and powerful force for profitability and a critical trigger for employee discretionary effort. It is real but unseen, and at the present time, there is no measure for emotional commitment. When tapped, it resolves unsolvable problems and creates cooperation and collaboration among team members. An employee's commitment to an organization develops over time. To understand how commitment develops, we need to look at the stages and the normative experience each individual and organization goes through to develop a long-term,

> Employees who emotionally commit to the organization are enthusiastic and zealous about their work.

committed relationship. Not everyone will agree on the stages, and not everyone goes through all stages.

In developing these relationship stages, we acknowledge the foundational work of the Relationship Institute's "Stages of Committed Relationships" (2015). The following stages represent a sustainable paradigm for building committed relationships within organizations.

Stage 1 – Potential. The potential stage is the recruitment stage that consists of attracting the right candidates, discerning the match, and hiring the employee. On the other end of the relationship, the potential employee also assesses the organization to determine if it is the right place with the right support to realize that individual's potential. The potential stage culminates in the company hiring the employee.

Stage 2 – Honeymoon. The honeymoon stage is the initial period of enthusiasm or goodwill, typically at the start of a new job. Discretionary effort or pre-emotional commitment discretionary effort is freely given by the employee. People go above and beyond what is required. They contribute and they feel good about themselves. This stage is characterized by feelings of excitement, enthusiasm, opportunity for self-development, and receptivity to expectations. The employees at this stage speculate they can offset any negative impressions of the company.

Stage 3 – Reality. While the honeymoon can last longer, it is usually a six-month period and is the shortest phase of developing a long-term relationship. Reality is seeing things as they are, not as you want them to be, or what they should be. The employee sees things as they are, and the employer fully perceives the employee's strengths and limitations. The employee will become aware of the implicit social contract and will feel the pressure to conform and be socially acceptable. When adjusting, the employee will limit discretionary effort to fit in.

> Authentic leaders unlock the discretionary effort of employees on a regular basis.

This stage also offers managers a chance to see the existing implicit social contract with new eyes. The relationship experiences disagreements and doubts as the individuals learn to adapt, deal with, and support their differences. Similarly, organizations will have to deal with the reality of the individual's capabilities, disagreements, expectations, and work with individuals to keep them in a mental state favorable to the company. This is where the authentic relationship that unlocks discretionary effort really begins.

Stage 4 – Disconnecting. As the reality stage sets in, there emerges in the employees' minds more disconnect between themselves and others in the organization. Typically, the employee does not share these disconnects but conducts an internal dialog of disagreement and argument with the way things are done. The engagement is now a daily power struggle. This is a typical stage in the development of a long-term committed relationship. Also in this stage, an employee may talk about leaving the company, for doubts arise, and regular feelings of ambivalence, anger, blame, and accusation become the normal internal dialog.

On the other side, leadership begins to talk about the employee leaving the company. Daily encounters become energy-draining and confusing. The initial reaction is to label and control the employee. A process they have used before of weeding out the 'bad" employees begins as the manager tends to keep the employee out of certain conversations.

At this stage, instead of cutting an employee out of conversations or threatening termination, the manager and employee should work together to explore what causes the feeling of disconnect. The employee should feel free to identify systemic, disagreeable issues in the organization itself. After evaluation of the issues, they can work together to eliminate the problems and turn the disgruntled employee into a valuable asset.

Stage 5 – Disengagement. Disengagement increases with the length of time that the relationship exists without conversations that address the hidden issues. Employers struggle with what to do with employees in this stage. Are they deadbeats that need to be forced do their jobs or potential diamonds in the rough that need support? The struggle is physically, mentally, and emotionally draining.

The task for the authentic leader is to stay the course, to keep working on cultivating and evaluating the potential of the employee.

It is about honoring the value employees bring to the organization in skills, education, and personal character gifts. This does not mean giving into the disengagement or being nice, rather it means confronting the disengagement openly, authentically, and helping work through the triggers of disengagement. The task for employees is to make a decision to stay present and honor their commitment or leave the organization. Because the grass is always greener on the other side of the fence, employees must be encouraged to look at the organization objectively with all its strengths and weaknesses.

There will be casualties within the organization. Some employees will stay for the wrong reasons and others will be willing to adapt and go forward. Some will leave either by their own choice or because management chooses. If both sides decide there is value in pursuing a forward course, they reach the next stage and become the grist upon which the organizational discretionary effort is built.

Stage 6 – Harmony. When employees and their management are in a state of harmony, they agree on a path forward. Harmony is the basis of a sustainable, committed professional relationship yet there are more profound meanings.

> A state of harmony between an employee and an authentic leader pushes progress.

In art and design, harmony is the visually satisfying effect of combining similar, related elements. This involves the skillful combination of colors from the color wheel or grouping of similar shapes to form an intriguing presentation, be that a piece of art or architecture. The world of music uses chords or the sounding of more than one pitch at a time to create harmony.

Harmony in art and music apply to business organizations. When employees and managers both understand their jobs, differences, strengths and weaknesses, and points of view, harmony happens. The "sounds" now created are discussions of opportunities for organizational and individual growth through collaboration and cooperation. At this stage, the relationship evolves toward an authentic, honest one.

Stage 7 – Optimization. Optimization is making the most effective use of resources, which for this discussion, implies unifying and using the resources all employees bring to the organization. For comparison, think of people living in the wilderness with no amenities: just as they make the best of every resource, an organization must also make the best of *every human resource*. When the organization is built on a foundation of trust and integrity and provides the essentials that employees need to be successful, it is in a state of optimization.

In the state of optimization, workers are absorbed in their tasks, find pleasure in their work, and exercise their best judgment at all times. Discretionary effort is at its peak. Team members do what they need to do at exactly the moment they are required to do it. Working with team members in a state of optimization is an enjoyable experience which motivates individuals to work even at great personal cost just for the shear sake of completing the project or assignment.

Working in a harmonious and optimized environment is so inviting that it provides the reason why employees struggle through the first stages of a committed relationship. Everyone wants to be on a winning team and in a winning organization. They want to add value, and when they do, they can leave work a little tired but elated at their accomplishments. If this happens regularly during the work week, people want to get up in the morning and look forward to their work day.

This stage-based example of relationship development explains the normal struggles organizations face as they seek emotional commitment from employees. It is a complex professional relationship process, but it is worthwhile to work toward a long-term committed relationships.

Commitment in the Eyes of Employees

While economic and physical rewards or the carrot and stick approach can motivate employees to produce on a daily basis, they are less effective than motivation built on emotional engagement. So how do managers enlist emotional commitment from employees? The answer begins at the base and progresses up through all levels of the RossBrandau Leadership Model. Employees must feel safe, accepted, welcomed and worthy. These dynamics of emotional commitment need to be met, not only through the first few weeks of employment, but on a regular basis throughout every week and month of employment. After feeling safe and accepted, employees need the following factors to be met as they make the decision to give emotional commitment:

- Desire to belong to the organization. Employees must be attracted to the explicit and implicit social culture of the company.
- Agreement with the vision and mission for the company. Create one that is engaging, meaningful, and implementable.
- Rational alignment with the goals, objectives and strategies of the company. Cascade the goals and objectives throughout the organization so they reach all levels of employees.
- Support in working through the stages of emotional commitment. Employees may not know they are going through the stages of emotional commitment. A savvy manager can assist them through the stages to harmony and optimization.
- Satisfaction in the work. Help employees find meaning and personal fulfillment in the work they produce and their contributions.

Emotionally committed workers exercise responsible autonomy or self-control, reducing required supervision and producing gains in efficiency. They move away from the 20th century social contract of a "fair day's work for a fair day's pay," and replace it with an understood social contract of giving discretionary effort. Implementing these leadership strategies make getting emotional commitment from employees predictable and more effective than a leadership style based on reward and coercive power.

The Real Question

When you have moved past mere engagement and have succeeded in gaining emotional commitment from employees, the real question is this: are they presently, at this moment in time, emotionally committed to your organization?

Organizations can't mandate emotional commitment in the employee handbook. It can't be a part of an employee's job description. Yet the path of gaining emotional commitment is a more effective leadership style than one based on reward and coercive power. To produce emotional commitment requires a daily investment of time and energy to connect with employees. It is the work of managers to give employees the choice to give the company emotional commitment and discretionary effort, both of which lead to authentic contribution. The dividends of the effort to give employees a genuine choice are endless in terms of worker energy, ideas, and creativity.

The Practice of Discretionary Effort

LEADERSHIP OF ONE
POWERFUL PRINCIPLE

Leadership of One Power Principle: Be the leader people choose to follow by developing objectivity.

Reflection

Emotional commitment is a different path for each individual. Leaders who understand the stages of commitment can help those around them achieve a more committed state sooner rather than later.

Every day you will meet employees in different stages of their emotional commitment to the organization. They don't walk in and say, "I am in Stage 3—reality is setting in—and I need your help." Instead, they walk in with a confusing array of messy emotional issues that are not easily resolved. They may have emotional issues plaguing their minds: *I'm not getting along with my boss the way I thought I would, my teammates aren't giving me enough explanation about the project, I'm not sure I approve of the direction this company is heading since I was hired.* Even if you are quick enough to identify the stage an employee is in, this does not mean you are adequately prepared to successfully deal with that individual at that stage.

As employees travel through the states of emotional commitment, objectivity on the part of the leader is important. An objective leader overlooks certain undesirable emotions by seeing the unique gifts the individual offers to the organization. As the manager and the employee work through difficult situations and negative emotions together, the employee becomes more emotionally committed and loyal to the manager and the organization. The process releases discretionary effort by the employee and turns the employee into a competitive advantage for the organization.

A variety of skills are needed to relieve some of the pain being felt by the employee. The challenge is to get through the situation and to move through the negative to the positive. The path forward is not always clear and it is not linear. Objectivity is a tool that will help leaders be patient with employees as they journey throughout the stages of emotional commitment.

Discretionary Effort Exercise:

Be Objective

Being objective as you or an employee move through the stages of emotional commitment allows you to commit to resolving the issue in the most effective way. When a negative emotional situation occurs, being objective involves looking at the solution and not getting caught in the problem. As you work with the individual to resolve a problem blocking emotional commitment, you are undoubtedly releasing your own individual discretionary effort.

Objectivity is challenging. It is difficult seeing "reality" or another viewpoint when we are in one of the stages or dealing with employees who are in various stages of emotional commitment. To be objective, observe what is happening without judgment and without micromanaging. If you feel judgmental or feel the need to fix the situation, just register these feelings internally. Put them on the shelf so that you can continue to observe objectively what is happening in an attempt to give neutral, non-blaming, and insightful feedback.

To be objective, be quiet and listen, stay alert to nonverbal cues, and remain open to different perspectives. Develop the ability to listen to all sides, the good and the bad, before taking action that is fair and balanced. Work to connect with the employee with your heart as well as your head. These tactics will help you create order out of disorder.

Discretionary Effort Practice Steps

Step 1: Observe and Experience. In the course of your day be mindful of remaining objective in every situation. Ask yourself what is the problem? What emotions are involved? Work to look at the situation in an unbiased way.

Step 2: Contemplate and Record. Maintain a record of your experiences of observing emotions within the workplace and the role of being objective.

Step 3: Share, Learn and Model. After you have evaluated the following questions, share your insights and ask for input from a mentor, a friend or trusted advisor.

1. What personal breakthroughs did I have when observing my own emotions? What caused any emotional breakdowns I experienced? Was I able to be objective?
2. What breakdowns did I observe with my direct reports, with colleagues, or in the organization in general? What breakthroughs did I observe as people in the organization dealt with emotional reactions to problems?
3. What is the relationship between being objective and discretionary effort?
4. How will I model being objective in the workplace? How will I assess if it works as a strategy for discretionary effort?

Reference

Relationship Institute. (2015, January 14). *The stages of committed relationships*. Retrieved http://relationship-institute.com/the-stages-of-committed-relationships/

CHAPTER 11

Leadership Level 5: Authentic Contribution

"We're like blind men on a corner—we have to learn to trust people or we'll never cross the street."
~ George Foreman

RossBrandau Discretionary Effort Leadership Model

PROFITABILITY AND ECONOMIC SUSTAINABILITY

- Authentic Contribution
- Emotional Commitment
- Rational Alignment
- Social Acceptance
- Safety and Security

WORK ENVIRONMENT OF INTEGRITY AND GRATITUDE

Figure 11.1: Leadership Level 5, Authentic Contribution

Just as people in organizations struggle with integrity, they also struggle with being authentic and understanding what authentic contribution means. Leadership Level 5 describes authentic and transparent behaviors and how they affect the integrity of the organization.

Karla had lunch with a friend; we'll call her Marci. As Marci sat across the table, Karla told her she was including authentic contribution in a new book on leadership. Karla asked Marci what authentic contribution meant to her. She looked at her food for a minute, raised her head, and proceeded to tell Karla about her new job and her hiring experience.

Marci and her husband had been in Dubai but wanted to come back to the States. Her husband found a job quickly, but it was taking her some time and a great deal of effort. Finally, she located a job she would enjoy, and she knew she had a wide array of toolsets that would allow her to execute this job in an excellent way. She made it through the first two interviews. Because it was a small business, the last interview was with the owner.

They had a pleasant conversation about her skills and her qualifications for the job. Then came the tough question: Why did you come back to the states? My friend paused, aware that her answer could limit her chances to be hired.

Deciding to be transparent, she answered, "We want to have a baby. We are experiencing infertility problems, and we needed to utilize the infertility expertise here in the United States."

She waited for, "Thank you very much for applying. We'll be in touch." To her surprise, the owner said, "I am so sorry to hear you are having problems. My sister had the same challenge." Their discussion lasted one hour. He hired Marci and supported her efforts to have children.

In that meeting, Marci demonstrated her authenticity. She was transparent and truthful in her interactions with the owner and did not hide her true commitment to a future family. In the owner's mind, there was no question that she would give authentic contributions in her work. In Marci's mind, there was no question whether she would give authentic contribution to this leader and his business.

Marci and her boss illustrate Leadership Level 5, Authentic Contribution—the top of the pyramid as shown in Figure 11.1. This level is where your valued employees take ownership for all they do and treat your business like their own. Most people don't make the move up the pyramid in the same manner that Marci did. For most it is a process, but at this level, employees take on the attitude of partners even though they do not have the title, the position of authority, or the big paycheck.

Some employees will never reach Level 5, but for those that do, they lead other employees regardless of their place on the organizational chart. When they have expertise, they lead. The leadership team permits this even if it means that the "leaders" will be the followers in certain circumstances.

Understanding Personal Authenticity

Are you authentic in your interactions with others in the workplace? Do you understand how to become authentic? In an article in *Psychology Today* written by Ronald Riggio, Ph.D., four components of being an authentic leader are identified. These components apply to everyone in the workforce, not just current leaders and managers.

First, the authentic person is self-aware. This implies a knowledge and understanding of your personal emotional intelligence, your values, and your strengths and limitations as discovered in assessments. As Shakespeare challenged five centuries ago, "Know thyself." Second, authentic people are transparent and genuine in their dealings with other people. Being genuine means abandoning hidden agendas and refusing to play games. Third, an authentic person is objective. We previously discussed objectivity in Chapter 10. Riggio terms this balanced processing or being fair-minded. To be an effective team player or leader means you solicit discussion and consider opposing viewpoints before making a decision. Fourth, an authentic person has an ethical core. As we pointed out in Chapter 2, having an ethical core means you do the right thing, the next right thing and do things right.

Understanding how to become authentic is harder than identifying authentic characteristics. Most people in the workplace struggle with being authentic because it takes courage. It requires resolve to live true to personal convictions and to speak up in meetings and conversations with your honest opinions, knowing you might be ridiculed.

Creating an environment where people can be authentic is the purpose of the RossBrandau Leadership Model. When you make people feel safe and secure, socially accept them, and rationally align them, you are creating a communication friendly environment where employees can overcome disconnection and achieve harmony. The ultimate reward is the creation of a human-led value culture where authentic people can thrive and contribute in a myriad of ways.

Owner Versus Renter Mentality

> Authenticity empowers and releases an internal energy that can be observed as discretionary effort.

Marci's story and the components of personal authenticity demonstrate the ideals of an employee who authentically contributes; this ideal can be summed up as an "owner's attitude." Marci did not go to work every day to do a job as if she was a renter, she went to work as an owner of her job, knowing she had a role to play in making the company prosperous.

Authentic means trustworthy, without deception, genuine, not counterfeit. It is not just for senior level positions, but it is for every position in the company regardless of the pay scale or level of responsibility. Employees with an authentic mindset take ownership of their individual stewardship in the company and work as if they are co-owners, careful with resources, and exhibit a work ethic that goes the extra mile to give discretionary effort. They have a sense of serving the customer, helping other employees, and facilitating the success of the company.

Owners accept full responsibility for their actions and their contributions that lead to a project's success. They believe deeply in the mission of the company, readily collaborate with others, and hold themselves and other team members accountable. Employees with the owner mentality realize that every day is a journey, and they join together as workers to undertake the new challenges of the adventure ahead. The owner's mentality includes several qualities:

- Reliable
- Respectful
- Grounded in the marketplace reality
- Willing to share information
- Able to let direct reports have authority
- Inspirational to other workers

The effect of being authentic is magnetic. Authentic people attract others and become a leader people choose to follow regardless of their status in the organization. As a leader of choice, they lead where others cannot, create combined energy, and figuratively link arms with the leadership team to fight for the survival of the company.

Finding employees who can advance to an authentic contributor status may seem like the search for the impossible dream that ends in frustration. You don't need to search far. A good place to start is by looking for current workers who are possibly stuck in disconnect and disengagement. Focus on these employees and help move them into states of harmony and optimization. Some employees will never mature to this point in the pyramid. They stubbornly hang onto the renter attitude of, "Oh, that is not my problem." With this attitude, a "renter worker" will not take part in tasks that are not specified in the job description. People with this mentality never build a career; they just work a job for their entire life.

> The authentic leader creates synergistic energy. They take people where others cannot.

Renters create a sustained strain on morale and innovation. The more owners you and your leadership team can develop will result in a release of discretionary effort from employees and greater financial rewards to the organization. When employees work as if they own the business, the business flourishes even in hard economic times.

The Whole is Greater Than the Sum of the Parts

Authentic contributors develop the ability to collaborate and work together with the organization to create new alternatives and new paths forward. Collaboration permits the creation of something that did not exist in the past. The process involves unleashing, releasing, and giving free reign to the creative powers in individuals as they increase trust, and develop and work as a team toward the goals of the organization.

Anyone who has worked with a team for an extended length of time has undoubtedly experienced the miracle of synergy. Synergy means that the sum of the collective whole is greater than the sum of its individual parts; the team playing as one achieves more than does the team playing as individuals. Synergy exceeds mathematical fact and makes it possible to add (1 + 1) = 3. Think of it another way: visualize carrots, flour, sugar, butter, oil and vanilla. Would you rather eat each ingredient separately or as a carrot cake? The cake represents the truth that was coined centuries ago by the philosopher Aristotle who said that the whole is greater than the sum of its parts.

Authentic contributors are less protective of their thoughts, less afraid someone will take credit for their work, and more ready to share their ideas. They know their idea could be a jumping off point for collaboration on an amazing new product or offering. They are less adversarial, defensive, and political while being more open and trusting.

In a collaborative session, someone puts an idea on the table, and it is not judged. Everyone gives suggestions for improvement. The product may look entirely different than it did at the beginning, but it doesn't matter to anyone as long as they see the new product as morphing into something that will be excellent when taken to market. Authentic contributors are willing to let their raw idea for a new product or service be taken by the "hands" of another who will mold it into the final masterpiece.

Some people have not experienced true collaboration because they have worked in an environment where ideas are squashed as silly, unworkable, or impractical. They have worked in a hierarchical environment where they were supposed to endorse the ideas of the ranking managers.

Karla experienced true collaboration when she served as the president of a local association in her professional field. The board had agreed to rework the association's bylaws at the annual planning retreat. As the discussion of the bylaws progressed, there were moments of intense bickering as several members of the leadership team had come with their own preconceived ideas of what they wanted to change. Definite sides were taken with lines figuratively drawn in the sand.

After one terse exchange there was dead silence. Then one member in a quiet voice expressed how getting this process right was a huge step forward to the growth of the association. She then summarized the bylaws discussion with four relevant ideas that had the potential of bringing both sides together. Her next step was to ask for critical feedback. She literally asked the other board members to make her ideas better. There was an immediate change in the charged atmosphere as the other board members recognized her courage and transparency. Egos slipped out the door.

Without being asked, others began sharing their experiences with the association and their insights, even some of their self-doubt. Rather than present their ideas in a spirit of "accept my idea or I'll take my marbles and go home," they fed on each other's insights and ideas and started to create a whole new scenario as to what the new bylaws would look like and how they could guide the association. As the process unfolded, a sense of maturity, substance, stability, and cohesion characterized this synergistic experience.

This is an example of the process of authentic contribution. The one member who spoke up was the leader everyone chose to follow. She was not the leader of the organization but she was the owner of the solution. She displayed transparency and objectivity. Think about your next event, whether it's a retreat or a staff meeting, and the impact this kind of collaboration could have on generating new ideas and the process to make those ideas better.

To try the process, give your leadership team or a few employees you consider to be authentic contributors a specific problem or challenge. Predictably, at the beginning of the facilitation, you will hear careful and measured statements as various alternatives and possibilities are explored. If you share ideas in an authentic way and ask the team to make your ideas better, others will follow your lead. You will experience a spontaneous "piggybacking" of ideas as people speak with courage and give you genuine feedback. You will have an experience where the heart and mind unite to drive your organization forward.

The Case for Intrapreneurs

There is a familiar maxim in the field of training and development: The CFO asks the CEO, "What happens if we invest in developing our people and then they leave us?" The CEO responds, "What happens if we don't and they stay?"

After authentic contributors learn to collaborate, a natural step forward is to encourage entrepreneurial thinking and to help authentic contributors develop into company entrepreneurs, frequently referred to as intrapreneurs. Intrapreneurs are entrepreneurs who work within a larger system. Being entrepreneurial entails taking initiative that typically involves risk. Entrepreneurs are usually identified as business owners. Intrapreneurs are not business owners in the same way, but they can play the same role of innovating if their company gives them the freedom to do so.

When intrapreneurs are given a budget for new projects, company time to experiment, and a generous allowance for mistakes, they will generate new concepts and designs for future products and services. The collaboration of intrapreneurs requires the technology and formal structure for capturing ideas, evaluating and deciding on the most profitable one, and finally starting the process of turning the ideas into reality.

Intrapreneurship and organizational learning are the keys to helping leadership teams deal with the strong headwinds of the marketplace in the next decade. Companies face more difficult environments for growth as they fight talent shortages, rapid technology changes, and global competition; they need new competitive advantages. A company has a competitive advantage when it is able to learn more quickly than its competitors. Organizational learning requires authentic contributors who are willing to share their expertise and knowledge while mentoring others in the development of innovative, entrepreneurial thinking.

Encouraging the development of entrepreneurial thinking and allowing authentic contributors to become intrapreneurs accelerates the journey to a full-fledged 21st century company. One of the most stimulating environments for intrapreneurial thinking is to create an unrestricted access to customers' compliments, complaints, and suggestions. This overcomes working in a vacuum where products are built that the hypothetical customer should like but will not purchase. With the ability to research customer feedback, intrapreneurial thinkers will find out why customers purchase the organization's products and services or why they prefer a competitor's. The authentic contributors who become intrapreneurs can refine current product features that give customers the results they want.

Authentic contributors who have an intrapreneurial mindset are an important part of making changes quickly, developing new ideas, and maintaining a competitive edge. They keep your company vibrant, so compensate them fairly and keep them close to your leadership team.

An Organization of Self-Motivated Workers

Are you asking, "All this theory sounds good, but how will this play out in my organization?"

Intrapreneurs are cost-effective ways to increase productivity and innovation.

Having the ability to create a vibrant company, an elite organization that grows authentic contributors with an intrapreneurial mindset, is a unique achievement. However, more and more corporations are finding that choosing to become an organization where superior, authentic relationships exist and workers are self-motivated is the only way to keep top talent and excel in markets that grow more competitive every day.

Successfully becoming an organization of self-motivated workers demands an environment where employees can transform into authentic contributors by performing satisfying work and being rewarded for their contributions. It means giving self-motivated personnel the freedom to become partners in innovating products and services, causing organic growth for the organization.

If management gives self-motivated people the right support, leadership emerges from individuals at every level in the organization and in all job functions. Finding self-motivated workers and giving them permission to become intrapreneurs is a cost-effective way to increase productivity and innovation. As they move from rational alignment and through the stages of emotional commitment to become authentic contributors, the organization thrives and experiences economic sustainability.

The Practice of Discretionary Effort

LEADERSHIP OF ONE
POWERFUL PRINCIPLE

Leadership of One Power Principle: Be the leader people choose to follow by being authentic and transparent.

Reflection

Achieving the state of authentic contribution paves the way for continual improvement, profitability, and economic sustainability. At this level, employees can operate in intrapreneurial ways as owners, not just renters. In the highest level of the RossBrandau Leadership Model, creativity, innovation, and collaboration are standard operating procedures and discretionary effort aligns with the organization's goals.

The leadership team can improve the number of employees who rise through the pyramid to authentic contribution if they project authenticity themselves. Authentic comes from the Greek word *authentikos* meaning "original, genuine, and principal," and from *authentes* "one acting on one's own authority." Each of us has an authentic self. This true self has an original way of expressing itself. Before looking for it in others, you must know more about *your* authentic self in order to understand your unique talents and value for the organization. Knowing your authentic self will pave the way for your own authentic contribution.

Discretionary Effort Exercise:

Listen for Authenticity

One way to discover authenticity is to listen to the way others talk about themselves. For example, an individual we interviewed obtained a promotion with a company within the corporation. When we talked over lunch a couple of months later, he explained his difficulty with the new position: the person he replaced had interpreted the standard performance metrics in a false way to make it look like the company division was getting superior results when they were not. His first goal in the new division was to surface the truth. He said, "If you don't know the truth, you don't know where to start or what to work on to improve outcomes. Deception destroys people systems and companies." To tackle the problem, he found employees who told the truth and started working with them. His words revealed his character and who he was as an authentic leader.

As you realize that what people say to you reveals their true feelings about themselves, you can analyze your own self-talk and uncover true feelings about yourself that may be hidden beneath the façade of your smile. Your self-talk will be aligned with how you view your authentic self.

Discovering your authentic self is not a linear development but a continuous process of getting closer to fully understanding your strengths, contributions, and value. Being authentic is not being good or right but is the willingness to discover your strengths and confront your weaknesses.

The focus of this assignment is to listen in an authentic way to the truth people tell themselves when they speak because self-talk becomes a self-fulfilling prophecy. As you gain an expertise in reading other people's self-talk, you will become aware of your own self-talk and the authentic self it reveals.

Every time people start explaining something to you, practice saying "listen for the authenticity." You will begin to understand the way they see themselves. As this picture emerges, you will make sense of their behaviors and actions. You will also become aware of the truth you tell yourself and this starts your journey toward authenticity.

Discretionary Effort Practice Steps

Step 1: Observe and Experience. In the course of your day, listen on a deeper level to what others say. Be aware that they are first and foremost talking to themselves. When they have a solution, they have told themselves it is a solution before they tell you. When they verbalize feelings of inadequacy or talk to you about a mistake they made, perhaps they are telling themselves that they are incompetent. By listening, you will detect their authentic self.

Step 2: Contemplate and Record. In a search for discovering the authentic self of employees, maintain a record of your experiences of listening to the truth that people speak; thus, you will gather clues on how to motivate your employees. Also, record the authentic truths you speak about yourself.

Step 3: Share, Learn and Model. After you have evaluated the following questions, share your insights and ask for input from a mentor, a friend, or a trusted advisor.

1. What breakthroughs did I have when I contemplated my authentic self? What breakdowns did I experience as I listened to the truth I was telling myself?
2. What breakthroughs did I have as I listened to the authentic truths people were revealing about themselves in our conversations? What breakdowns in authenticity did I observe as I worked with individuals?
3. What is the relationship between the truth people tell themselves and discretionary effort?
4. How do I plan to become a more authentic individual and a more authentic leader?

Reference

Riggio, R. (2014, January 22). What is authentic leadership? Do you have it? *Psychology Today online*. Retrieved from https://www.psychologytoday.com/blog/cutting-edge-leadership/201401/what-is-authentic-leadership-do-you-have-it

CHAPTER 12

Profitability and Economic Sustainability

"Globalization has left only one true path to profitability for firms operating in high-wage, developed nations: to base their competitive strategy on exceptional human capital management. Any benefits that, historically, have been associated with superior technology and access to capital (both financial and physical) are now too fleeting to provide sustainable advantage. The most competitive companies will be those that manage their employees like the assets they are."
~ Laurie Bassi & Daniel McMurrer

RossBrandau Discretionary Effort Leadership Model

PROFITABILITY AND ECONOMIC SUSTAINABILITY

Authentic Contribution

Emotional Commitment

Rational Alignment

Social Acceptance

Safety and Security

WORK ENVIRONMENT OF INTEGRITY AND GRATITUDE

Figure 12.1: Beyond the leadership levels to profitability and sustainability

A business definition for economic sustainability is using various company assets efficiently to allow the company to continue functioning in the profit mode over time. To be blunt, "economic sustainability [is] the business of staying in business" (Doane and MacGillivray 2001).

Previously, there has not been a balanced approach to profitability. Profitability, as stated by Bassi and McMurrer, was largely based on superior technology and access to capital. This book and the entire RossBrandau Discretionary Effort Leadership Model are an essential study for 21st century leaders because of the emphasis on people and a human-led culture which is the surest path toward company profitability and economic sustainability.

There is no standard recipe and no one-size-fits all solution to corporate success. It is a custom-made process of defining corporate profitability and economic sustainability in terms that match your product development, current market positioning, vision of the future, and existing challenges. The leadership team is ultimately responsible for the performance of the organization. As the leaders drive toward continued profitability and economic sustainability, cultivating the interdependency of employees in collaborative interactions is a strategy that produces results. As shown in Figure 12.1, the five leadership levels pave the way to interdependency, collaboration, and the ultimate employee gift of authentic contribution.

Individual Profitability and "The Zone"

For a company to have economic stability, individuals within the company must be profitable, meaning they need to contribute on a daily basis in a way that keeps the company in the black. This is why it is imperative for individuals in a company to refine their time management skills, so they are productive every day. When each individual in the company completes tasks on a daily basis that contributes to profitability, takes responsibility for fixing problems, and suggests improvements––in other words, functioning as an authentic contributor--the company is in a position to experience economic stability.

In the sports world, there is a term that is used when athletes individually perform at their best ability and make incredible authentic contributions to the team. The term is "playing in the zone." An athlete who consistently plays in the zone achieves recognition, is in demand and can require a higher salary. In the world of professional athletics, the team with the most players in the zone will have more wins than losses, which provides profitability and economic sustainability to the franchise.

Most athletes don't talk about the zone, but when asked, they can tell you what it means to play in the zone. NBA star, Bill Russell described being in the zone when he played basketball with the Boston Celtics:

> "When it happened, I could feel my play rise to a new level. It came rarely, and would last anywhere from five minutes to a whole quarter, or more. Three or four plays were not enough to get it going. It would surround not only me and the other team, but even the referees. At that special level, all sorts of odd things happened: The game would be in the white heat of competition, and yet somehow I wouldn't feel competitive, which is a miracle in itself. I'd be putting out the maximum effort, straining, coughing up parts of my lungs as we ran, and yet I never felt the pain. The game would move so quickly that every fake, cut, and pass would be surprising, and yet nothing could surprise me. It was almost as if we were playing in slow motion.... There have been many times in my career when I felt moved or joyful, but these were the moments when I had chills pulsing up and down my spine. (1979)"

Playing in the zone requires discipline and practice of fundamental skills on a daily basis. When added to physical health, a positive mental attitude, and proper warmup on game day, playing in the zone can be a frequent occurrence instead of an aberration. In similar manner, employees are like professional athletes. Having a substantial output of tasks and decisions that move the company forward takes discipline to identify the urgent and vital tasks to be completed for the day, good physical health, the right attitude, and the skills to execute. When these elements come together for an employee, that employee can be considered to be "working in the zone." It is amazing what a large number of employees working in the zone can do for a company.

Although the phenomenon of playing in the zone is primarily attributed to athletes, it can happen for any professional intent on a goal. You may have witnessed an athlete who played in the zone or you may have experienced playing in the zone as a participant in an athletic contest. Once you understand the concepts, you can apply the principles of being in the zone to your work life. For example, Russell's description that nothing could surprise him during zone-level performance can be related to an experienced employee who sees a situation, knows what needs to happen, and takes the requisite or the required action to resolve the issue—all before others have time to analyze the situation. Working in the zone means personal performance rises to new levels of excellence, perhaps to a pinnacle of employee's ability to achieve.

The zone is also known as flow. Flow is the mental state of high performance that is experienced by people in all areas of discipline. Daniel Goleman and Mihaly Csikszentmihaly are two researchers who have looked at the effect of flow on the human mind. Goleman reports, "New research is leading to the conclusion that these instances of absorption are, in effect, altered states in which the mind functions at its peak, time is often distorted and a sense of happiness seems to pervade the moment" (1986).

> Working in the zone or the flow state is the ultimate state of productivity.

Authentic contributors often find themselves working in the zone or in a state of flow. Flow is experienced as the suspension of time, the freedom of complete absorption in activity. It is one of the most enjoyable and valuable experiences a person can have at work. People feel fully immersed in a feeling of energy, engagement, and enjoyment in the process of the activity. In his research on happiness, Csikszentmihaly concluded that people are the happiest at these times when they are stretching themselves to achieve something. It is in these times they feel in control of their actions and masters of their fate. Csikszentmihaly's book *Flow: The Psychology of Optimal* identified the ten factors that create the state of flow within an individual:

1. **Clear goals.** The expectations and rules are discernible and goals are attainable and align appropriately with one's skill set and abilities.
2. **Balance between ability level and challenge.** The activity is neither too easy nor too difficult.
3. **Personal control.** There is a sense of personal control over the situation. Value is added by the individual.
4. **Direct and immediate feedback.** The successes and failures in the course of the activity are apparent, so that behavior can be adjusted as needed.
5. **Concentration.** There is a high degree of concentration on a limited field of attention so that a person engaged in the activity will have the opportunity to focus and to delve deeply into it.
6. **The merging of action and awareness.** There is a loss of the feeling of self-consciousness.
7. **Distorted sense of time.** One's subjective experience of time is altered.
8. **Less self.** There is a lack of awareness of ego and bodily needs.
9. **Focused on the moment.** People become absorbed in their activity, and focus of awareness is narrowed down to the activity itself, action and awareness merging.
10. **Intrinsically rewarded.** There is an effortlessness of action. You do it without external rewards.

> Create a clear vision – the WHY – of what the employee should do then let them figure out HOW to achieve the vision.

Each of these points are important productivity principles taken from either view: as an individual or as a manager. The first four points speak to management principles. As laid out in our discussion of Leadership Level 3, Rational Alignment, it is the responsibility of first, the company, second, the department, and then the manager to set goals, objectives and expectations. It is the manager's direct responsibility to ensure that the goals align with each employee's skill set, balancing the ability and the challenge involved. Once the assignment is clear and the "why" of the task is established, the manager should give the employee some personal control over the "how" the task is completed. Immediate feedback provides reassurance and encouragement during the task progression and course correction as needed. When the assignment is clearly made, the authentic contributor is free to take action with focused concentration and experience the almost out-of-body experience of working in the zone. The individual experiences a sense of well-being along with the intrinsic mental and emotional reward of feeling competent.

When employees work in the zone as authentic contributors, discretionary effort is unforced. It is effortless. A fascinating outcome of discretionary effort is discretionary *energy* which is an internal state of renewal as opposed to depletion. As a result of being in the zone, athletes are invigorated by the game and employees are revitalized by the intellectual challenge of production and creation. Extra energy is released and the individual experiences renewal of physical strength, attitudes, and emotions.

While focusing on the task at hand and experiencing working in the zone, authentic contributors can also become more aware of their environment and how their ultimate success is dependent upon those around them. Those working in the flow state or the zone will push for greater goal attainment from team members, coworkers, and colleagues thus achieving increased productivity and profitability for all. Sustainability is extended into the future.

This discussion of working in the zone is to connect the ideas of individual success and organization profitability. Profitability comes by having workers who consistently work in the zone. The attention to individual employees is what will make your company economically sound. The following sections help detail the benefits of helping each worker achieve zone-level performance, authentic contribution, and discretionary effort.

Two-Way Responsibility

Moving employees up the pyramid to become authentic contributors who know how to work in the zone means you create the human-led culture where people are valued for the hearts, minds, and thinking ability, not just their brawn. In a human-led culture of authentic contributors, employees and managers have a co-equal responsibility for productivity and profits. This responsibility is played out as a two-way street of communication and collaboration. The two-way street means the balance of power shifts between contributor and manager as the need for expertise changes. In the process, authentic contributions are made and discretionary effort is released. The table below summarizes the elements of 2-way communication.

Leadership/Manager Responsibility	Authentic Contributor Responsibility
From Employee to Valued Asset	
Continuous training and development of employees	Learn and clarify assignments
From Informal to Planning	
Steady planning with appropriate employee involvement	Contribute to the planning when expertise and insight are needed
From Power to Trust	
Proper delegation of responsibility and authority	Take responsibility for the job and be accountable
From Threats to Motivation	
Relevant follow-up, feedback, and praise	Complete work and report back

Figure 12.2: Qualities for leader/manager and employee collaboration

The bullet points below summarize some of the primary ways that leadership can advance communication and collaboration with all employees.

- **See employees as assets.** When leaders see employees as assets and invest in them, employees continue to increase in value. Conversely, employees need to take training for the purpose of learning and growing. When assigned a project, they have the responsibility to ask questions for clarification.
- **Build trust.** In our model of discretionary effort, trust means feeling safe and accepted. If employees feel safe with managers, they will share their thoughts and concerns about issues and offer solutions. Because employees are closer to the complications and glitches encountered on a daily basis, they should be brought into problem-solving discussions. This a significant step in developing discretionary effort.
- **Include employees in planning.** In the 20th century, management informed employees on a need to know basis. Withholding information is a critical mistake in today's world where knowledge moves at the speed of light, the fastest movement measurable. It is important to give employees the big picture or as much information as you can to enable them to make intelligent decisions when they come to crossroads. With big picture information, it is less likely they will veer off course but instead keep their sights on the goal. Pull the authentic contributors into your inner circle and use their brain power to keep setting and reaching your target goals. Mark Van Doren (n.d.), American poet and writer, said, "Bring ideas in and entertain them royally, for one of them may be the king." In every planning stage, listen to your authentic contributors—one of them may have the royal idea that will catapult you ahead of your competition.

- **Share power.** Some people carefully guard power, thinking if they share it, they will lose it. Nothing could be farther from the truth. When you share power, the collective power expands. However, the greatest advantage to sharing power is that it turns employees into renewable energy like solar or wind power.

- **Motivate by removing blocks.** Motivation is as much about leaders removing the things that demotivate employees in the organization as it is about adding rewards that inspire action. As projects move forward, an important role of the leader is to ask, "What is stopping your progress?" If it is lack of statistics from human resources, financial information from accounting or sales literature from marketing, the leader can use influence to get the needed information. Sometimes, progress is slow on in-depth projects because of a lack of physical man hours. In this case, the manager can reassign tasks to other team members. The simple problems mentioned here can become huge distractions and be demotivating to authentic contributors. Removing them resets the individual's energy and self-motivation.

Mentoring Employees for Profitability

Figure 12.3 shows what typically happens when an employee is hired. As you can see, the interaction between the manager and the employee goes up together. The employee's ascent is a little steeper because each individual starts at a low level of knowledge about the organization but brings incredible enthusiasm to the new job.

A new job is a fresh start, and each new hire has high hopes of having meaningful work and being able to contribute. If a leader can remember the feelings of being a new employee, it will help in the mentoring process.

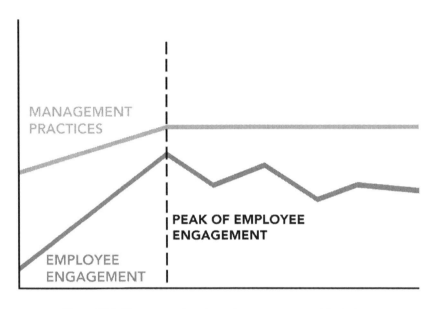

Figure 12.3: Management and employee engagement trajectory

After a certain amount of training, normally the manager's involvement with the employee lessens and perhaps becomes static as you can see by the Management Practices line. In the Employee Engagement line, you find the enthusiasm and engagement of the employee declines as the attention from the manager becomes static. The decline means the employee is not motivated to move up the pyramid to emotional commitment and authentic contribution. If the engagement of the employee continues to decline, the employee usually finds another job and leaves, taking intellectual property gained at the company out the door. Company money that should have counted as a profit is instead used in the hiring and training process of a new employee.

In the graph in Figure 12.4, we see that as a manager stays involved through the dips in an employee's engagement in the job, the manager can re-energize and motivate this source of renewable power: the employee. The manager mentors the employee through the five leadership levels: safety and well-being, social acceptance, emotional commitment, and rational alignment. The manager and the engaged employee progress together to authentic contribution as they become partners in the profitability and economic sustainability of the organization.

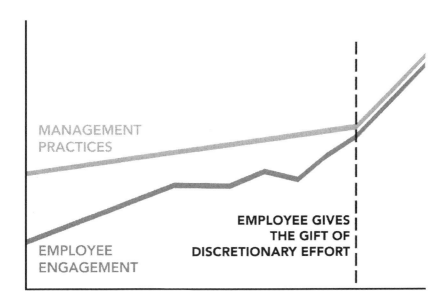

Figure 12.4: Employee growth when the manager stays involved

The People Payoff

There is one question that can evoke heated discussions in companies: are employees an expense or are they an investment? From an accounting standpoint, it is relatively easy to assign profitability to individual capital goods (machinery), funds, and technology. It is not as easy to determine the profitability generated by each individual in an organization or to measure human capital profits. Until the industrial revolution, land was the basis to measure profit. The revolution changed the focus to capital goods and technology, which served us well until about the 1980s. In the 20th century, it made sense to consider "return on capital" where that capital was not just land but financial investments and capital goods.

We are now in a knowledge economy and there is a growing need to measure the "profit per employee," the "people payoff" or the Return on People (ROP). To get the greatest ROP, move them through the pyramid levels, and encourage them to be authentic contributors. When you do, they become the creators of organizational wealth. It is worth the investment of your time and money to develop authentic contributors because the talented people who have the potential to reach Level 5 are relatively scarcer than capital or technology.

We recommend the people investment not be measured as a cost factor but as a value factor. Each person is an intangible asset that makes a value-added contribution every day to the efficiency and effectiveness of the organization's product or service. Recognizing this value connection, it makes sense to use a system of metrics that includes both money and human capital to measure profitability.

The 21st century marketplace is unpredictable and full of ambiguity. Predictable command and control methods, with their focus on structure and functions, scorecards, and hierarchical decision-making, restrict the exchange of information and do not provide the flexibility to adjust to market conditions in uncertain times. Increasingly being seen as 20th century processes, command and control methods are being replaced in progressive companies by a renewed respect for quality, culture, learning, diversity, and employee engagement, all of which earns the company the discretionary effort of employees.

In *Profit Beyond Measure,* H. Thomas Johnson and Anders Broms assert (2000):

> Managers can no longer accept without question the conventional wisdom that says an organization will reach its bottom-line goals best if it drives its employees to achieve financial targets which makes a manager's primary task to

exceed quantitative targets defined by the financial measures
set forth by the senior leadership team.

Johnson and Broms label this dated corporate behavior as
"managing by results" or managing by outcomes, which is the belief
that order, company processes, and the attainment of company
goals must be externally imposed on a division, unit, or team. Those
with production experience know that physical systems have
physical limits on the quality and quantity of what they produce.
Setting production objectives that exceed the system's means may
produce short-term results but inevitably degrade the system itself.
The same analogy can be made to setting team/employee targets
by the "external" senior leadership team with no input from the
employees performing the actual tasks.

Profit Beyond Measure makes the case that managing by results
leads to inefficiencies as employees mistakenly focus their work on
reaching their financial targets and quotas. Instead, the focus
should be on top-notch quality, needed innovation of products and
services and exceptional customer service. These more crucial
efforts are often put aside and replaced with the distracting
pressure of meeting the objectives determined by upper
management.

Johnson and Broms focus on quality match the words of
Edward Deming, who is considered the father of the quality
revolution. Deming also criticizes managing by results when he said,
"Focus on outcome [or management by results] is not an effective
way to improve a process or an activity. Management by numerical
goal is an attempt to manage without knowledge of what to do, and
in fact is usually management by fear" (2002). Higher operating
costs and suboptimal long-term profitability is the price of
managing by fear rather than cultivating systemic learning.
Systemic learning involves building the vision of quality inside the
employees and letting them determine the process or means to
achieve success, which we equate with "management by means."

Management by means is the opposite of managing by results.
Managing by means permits new directions and innovation to occur
by empowered workers who confront challenges and find solutions
on a daily basis. The RossBrandau Leadership Model is aligned with
managing by means in the belief that a desirable end emerges

naturally as a consequence of nurturing the growth of all employees.

Realizing that every organization cannot function without formal mission, values, vision, goals, and that these need to be put in place by the senior leadership team, we agree that moving to an environment founded on management by means is a must for profitability. The management by means places the emphasis on the individual worker and their ability to learn, share knowledge, and collaborate. The RossBrandau Leadership Model takes the management by means concept one step further because our model asks for leadership, not just management. It builds leaders who know how to manage by means AND who lead employees to authentic contributions. Individual workers are the only assets that when they are giving emotional commitment and authentic contribution become the foundational base of a company's competitive advantage in the 21st century marketplace.

The Practice of Discretionary Effort

Leadership of One Power Principle: Becoming the leader people choose to follow requires you to develop the discipline to work in the zone.

Reflection

In general, people like instances of performing in the zone even though they may not realize that is what is happening to them. Working in the zone allows the release of internal energy that creates new levels of excellence. It is a mental and emotional state of effort that gives you a feeling of energy, engagement, and enjoyment in the current activity.

We call this feeling discretionary effort with its accompanying discretionary energy. Usually this occurs when you are stretching yourself to achieve something. When you are experiencing the zone, you take responsibility for every action and stretch yourself to perform at higher levels and you often slip into it without even knowing why or how.

Becoming the leader people chose to follow means that first you need to experience "the zone" where discretionary effort is released and performance rises to new levels. From a company viewpoint, workers performing in the zone are the key to profitability and economic sustainability.

Discretionary Effort Exercise:

Be In the Zone

The purpose of this exercise is for you to recognize if you are in or out of the zone. The reason you do this is so that you can replicate the feeling of being in the zone more often and you can begin to realize what distracts you and takes you out of the zone.

Discretionary Effort Practice Steps

Step 1: Observe and Experience. In the course of your day become aware of when you are in the zone or flow and when you are not. Notice others who are in the zone. Notice what triggers put you into the zone and which distractions take you out.

Step 2: Contemplate and Record. Maintain a record of your observations of being in the zone.

Step 3: Share, Learn and Model. After you have evaluated the following questions, share your insights and ask for input from a mentor, a friend, or a trusted advisor.

1. What personal breakthroughs did I have about being in the zone at work? What were the triggers? Did I have any breakdowns that blocked being in the zone? What were the distractions that took me away from the zone?
2. What breakthroughs or breakdowns did I observe about the ability of my colleagues or team members to be in the zone?
3. What is the relationship between being in the zone and discretionary effort?
4. How will I model being in the zone in the workplace? How will I assess if it works as a strategy for discretionary effort?

5. Did I in any way experience the discretionary energy within myself? Did it fuel me, multiply my energy, and take me to another level of performance?

References

Csikszentmihaly, M. (1992). *Flow: The psychology of optimal experience*. New York: HarperPerennial.

Deming, W. E. (2002). *Out of the crisis*. Cambridge: Massachusetts Institute of Technology, Center for Advanced Engineering Study.

Johnson, H. T. & Broms, A. (2000). *Profit Beyond Measure.* NY: Free Press

Russell, B., & Branch, T. (1979). Second wind: the memoirs of an opinionated man. New York: Random House.

Goleman, D. (1986, March 4). Concentration is likened to euphoric states of minds. *New York Times*. p. 1.

Doane, D. & MacGillivray A. (2001 March). Economic sustainability: The business of staying in business. *R & D Report*. Retrieved from http://isites.harvard.edu/fs/docs/icb.topic140232.files/RD_economic_sustain.pdf

CHAPTER 13

The Essence of 21st Century Leadership: The Gift of Discretionary Effort

"The task of leadership is not to put greatness into people, but to elicit it, for the greatness is there already."
~ John Buchan

"Leadership is not about changing the mindset of the group, but in the cultivation of an environment that brings out the best and inspires the individuals in that group."
~ Arthur F. Carmazzi

Examine the two quotes above carefully. These quotes are a summary of the intent of this book: taking care of employees is taking care of business. When these attitudes are part of the mindset of your managers and employees respond, your employees become your competitive advantage.

Evaluate the messages from the paradigm of your personal leadership style. The paradigms that relate to 21st century leadership are:

1. Greatness resides in workers as their innate character gifts. A 21st century leader will create an environment and relationships that elicit the release of employee greatness in the form of discretionary effort.
2. A 21st century leader will bring out the best in the group by *inspiring* them to greater achievements.

Creating discretionary effort is an untapped, free resource that translates into increased energy of mind and body for the worker experiencing the phenomenon. It is solution-oriented energy that creates synergy in the organization, giving it the ability to reduce costs and increase market share.

A concept related to the creation of discretionary effort is a time management term: discretionary time. The term discretionary means available to be used when and how you decide. Being able to decide what to do in your own personal discretionary time is a powerful tool for self-esteem and feeling in control of your personal work life.

In contrast, however, employees don't *find* discretionary effort, they *give* discretionary effort. If the RossBrandau Leadership Model is in full operation in your company, when employees find discretionary time, they hopefully will give discretionary effort. Discretionary effort is available inside of each employee, and they use it when they desire to use it. Discretionary effort does not mean that employees put in extra hours to accomplish more work or that salaried employees do more work without additional pay. To the contrary, it is about employees being so focused, involved and interlaced with the organizational goals that they innately work more efficiently, creatively, and intuitively do what is right in the moment.

For many years, "engagement" has been the buzz word in organizations to achieve this kind of worker—"Let's get the employees engaged!" When compared to the power of discretionary effort, however, engagement is only a promise, a possibility that the employee will give discretionary effort. Engagement can be called potentiality which means, "A chance of possibility that something will happen or exist in the future; a quality that can be developed to make someone or something better" (Merriam-Webster, n.d.), but it is not the actual action of doing more, just a commitment to do more. Working to get employees to the point beyond commitment and rational alignment, into the actual delivery of discretionary effort, is the key to company success in the 21st century, for all your employees will outperform your competition.

Employees are Free to Choose

As we have stated in this book, employees are free to choose whether or not they will give discretionary effort. When employees walk through the door every morning, they make a simple yet profound decision that has unparalleled impact on the success of the organization. That decision is, "How hard am I going to work today?"

Do I immediately get to work or do I check the headlines online, do a little "chit-chatting" with my favorite gabby colleague? Do I answer the phone or do I let it go to voicemail? Do I immediately return the email asking for information or do I let it sit for several hours? Should I finish the assignment on time or ask for an extension? Should I tell my manager about an idea to cut costs or just close my eyes to the waste? Should I double check my completed work for possible errors or just send it on and hope no one finds any errors? It is all about individual choices every hour of the day.

When an employee does find discretionary time, they make a conscious decision, a free-will choice to give discretionary effort, that little extra not mandated by the formal signed contract. They decide to create value for the employer by doing things they don't really have to do, like staying late, coming in early, double checking the presentation for errors, inviting the new employee to lunch, promptly calling a customer back, or helping a colleague who is stuck on a problem. These little actions make a big difference in today's economy, where the most successful organizations succeed by creating an environment where employees freely give their ideas and opinions as well as demonstrate care, pride, and a sense of ownership in the business. Your workers' discretionary effort puts your company into a superior business position.

By nature, discretionary effort cannot be forced; employees must choose to give it through the exercise of free will. Free will is the ability of an individual to make an independent and voluntary decision, free from coercion and based on a course of action that fulfills a personal desire or need.

In most work environments, employees desire to do just enough to stay out of trouble. They see no purpose to choose to give more than the minimum acceptable level of effort. In contrast, in an environment focused on superior relationships, leadership teams work to establish trust, sustain morale, and build camaraderie in order to motivate employees to exercise their free will to consistently give a high level of discretionary effort.

Because an individual's discretionary effort is an optional, free-will choice, not everyone's contribution will be at the same level. There is a wide range of discretionary effort individuals offer to the organization. The range goes from the minimum acceptable to get an acceptable performance review to the maximum level of possible output that places them at the authentic contribution level. Here are some of the ways leaders can classify an individual's contribution:

1. **Immediacy.** How proactively does an employee voluntarily offer discretionary effort? Before any anticipated need, when the need arises, or never unless asked?
2. **Commitment.** How long-term or short-term is the individual's contribution? Are there short bursts only when the boss is looking? Or is it offered on a long-term basis as part of the work culture?
3. **Application.** Does the individual contribute discretionary effort for the right reasons, to further organizational strategies and tasks? Or is the individual pursuing his or her own goals and ambitions?

Each employee gives discretionary effort based on the skills they have acquired, the knowledge they have gained, and the level of expertise that has grown with their experiences throughout their employment. The role of the leadership team is pivotal for the organization. The creation of the environment where discretionary effort is regularly released requires consistency, continual work, and perseverance. The performance improvement strategy must recognize that each employee is a valuable resource capable of creating value beyond the obvious because a workforce of motivated individuals is the key to organizational survival in today's competitive marketplace.

Employees as Appreciating Assets

In Chapter 12, we discussed that in a standard accounting spreadsheet, a human being is counted as a liability, not a benefit. Leaders often struggle with fundamental questions such as "What is the value of each individual?" On one hand, people at certain levels are highly valued and are reimbursed accordingly. At other levels people have lower value and are reimbursed accordingly. Either way, business often treats people as liabilities, consumers of capital rather than as assets and producers.

People are complex, demanding, and more often than not, come with personal, medical, and family problems. Business routinely looks for ways to reduce its reliance on human beings, especially at the basic function areas in an organization. It comes as no surprise, then that when tough times happen, people are let go as a primary cost-reduction device.

What if, instead of seeing them as a liability on the spreadsheet, you were to see them as a resource that can give you a competitive edge in the marketplace on a daily basis? People add something that goes beyond scientific and engineering knowledge. When people are at the center of corporate growth, moving products and services to new levels, they become a key engine for progress and their creativity and ingenuity literally become your vital assets.

21st century leaders who want to see workers reach their potential ask these questions:

- "What is the best way to organize for success and increased growth at every level, while being mindful of the priorities and needs of individuals?"
- "How can we keep people from losing their enthusiasm in the daily chaos and/or the boring humdrum or routine details of work?"
- "How can we keep employees from becoming disconnected and burned out?"

- "How can we keep people informed, involved and participating in the priority-setting and the decision-making, thereby making them an important factor in the accountability process?"
- "What processes can we establish that make the very best use of our employees' individual talents?"

Finding the answers to these questions not only makes your employees indispensable for your success but also creates a human-led value organization. People will be at the center of the company, resulting in a more innovative culture and increasingly interesting work for employees.

Earning the Gift of Discretionary Effort

You and your competitors have access to the same equipment, the same materials, the same technologies and the same processes, but the organization that does the best job of maximizing the amount of discretionary effort given by their workers will win in the marketplace.

We have described in this book how to earn discretionary effort with strategic initiatives that include operating from a foundation of integrity, making employees feel safe and secure, being concerned with their total well-being, offering them social acceptance and giving them solid company mission, values, vision and goals to align with and follow.

With this foundation, consider these tactical tips:

Give them rough guidelines. If you give employees the WHY and point them in the right direction then let them figure out HOW, they can use their creativity and knowledge to innovate products and services. This process builds their self-esteem and gives them the opportunity to become an authentic contributor. When they surprise you with the results they have produced, acknowledge them. For managers, appropriate delegation clears your plate to concentrate on moving the unit, team or department forward. The employee, displaying their gifts through the giving of discretionary effort, gains intrinsic motivation and satisfaction, the true motivator.

When we consulted at Fort Benning in Columbus, Georgia, Karla had the opportunity to have lunch with the head of the Army Research Institute. He said, "You should see what happens when I bring young people into my office, describe a new project, and ask them if they would like to head the project up. When they get excited about taking on the project, I tell them that if it flies, they will get all the credit. If it bombs, I'll take the rap."

This man created huge amounts of discretionary effort by offering recognition and safety to individuals willing to take a risk and experiment, in essence, develop the entrepreneur inside. His employees were partnering with him and giving authentic contribution to the Army.

Allow release time for private projects. As part of their efforts to release discretionary effort to find innovative new products, 3M allows employees to schedule five hours a week to work on any project they want, research anything they want, and make mistakes. Google has had similar policies in the past. Knowing that it is OK to stretch and experiment without recrimination is one kind of safety that leads to discretionary effort. To this point, what changes are appropriate in your organization that would permit value creation by offering formal permission to allocate certain hours each week to a favorite project?

Plan time to brainstorm and collaborate. Sometimes the most valuable insights and innovations for an organization come about unexpectedly. Look at the results of some of the unstructured interactions between your managers and your employees. Is there a way to channel those results to encourage discretionary effort? If you are able to channel greater amounts of discretionary effort from your employees into achieving critical business objectives, your company will outperform the competition.

Reinforce the company's umbrella of direction. When you are in discussions with teams or individuals, you can increase discretionary effort by reinforcing the vision, mission and goals of the company. Reinforcement of company values helps employees stay in alignment with the firm's long range goals, assuming their personal goals are a fit. As you listen to employees, you can subtly ask questions that uncover their personal career goals and their life goals. Ask yourself if there is congruency between the company goals and what the employee tells you about her personal vision.

If employees' only motivator is money, it will be hard to get them to emotionally commit to the organization and enter the final stage of authentic contribution. However, if they are on board with the vision and mission of the company, they are well on their way to giving you discretionary effort, making valuable contributions to your company and becoming your most important resource.

Give them access to the right feedback at the right time. One young engineer Karla coached worked for an international company. He was five levels below the final decision maker, who lived in New York City. Being tasked to build a certain feature for a new product, he made a prototype and received good reviews from his immediate supervisor along with suggestions for a few changes. After he made the changes, they submitted the prototype up to the next level. Once again the product met the standards the up-line manager wanted and it was pushed to the next level. This review and revision process took nearly six weeks. At the end of reviews by various managers, the product was submitted to the final decision maker in New York. The final decision maker said the entire concept was wrong and demanded it be reworked completely. There were only two weeks to the drop-dead deadline, throwing everyone into total chaos.

If the worker, the inventor, was more closely connected to the decision-making manager in a more streamlined management structure, untold time, energy, frustration, and anger could have been avoided. So the question is: What kind of relationship will you establish in your organization between the person performing the actual work and the person signing off on it? As you create superior relationships built on discretionary effort, these situations will happen less frequently.

At the end of the 20th century and after the most recent recession, every business understands the motto, "Do more with less." In other words, your organization may have fewer resources, but you are still expected to do better than the last fiscal cycle. The only physical way your company can increase productivity is by having a higher number of workers or by having workers with a higher output. Financial balance sheets often dictate that you won't be able to hire more workers so you will need the employees you have to produce more work. An obvious way to do that is to create a workplace that earns the gift of discretionary effort.

One way of earning more discretionary effort can be found in the motto of "do more with less," but with a change in the meaning. Workers will do more with less top-down control and less pointless critiquing. A better motto could be, "See more, do more," or see the potential within your current workers who can be intrinsically motivated to give more discretionary effort. "See more, do more" can also mean that people will do more if you give them more vision and communicate with them more.

Think about what a difference you could make if you invested 15 to 30 minutes of your discretionary effort every day to encourage discretionary effort in others. Encouragement can be as elaborate as holding a meeting to brainstorm ideas with a specific team. It can be as simple as a casual conversation in the break room or a walk down the hall together. It can be anything that acknowledges the simple, everyday actions by the rank and file employee and lets the employee know, "I am grateful for your contributions." A 21st century leader creates a safe work environment, accepts people as they are, aligns resources for value creation, taps emotional power, and encourages authenticity to create genuine and sustainable discretionary effort.

Diluting Discretionary Effort

Unfortunately, there are a variety of ways that organizations can limit or dilute the value-added contribution, or discretionary effort, each employee has the potential to contribute, thereby limiting and constraining collective optimization. One way that leadership teams hold diluting power over discretionary effort is by placing people in positions that are not a good fit for their skill set.

When management randomly decides what benefits and perks individuals will receive without calibrating them from job to job, employees quickly recognize the injustices and inconsistencies. If there is little consistency in positions and benefits, employees limit their discretionary effort and are regularly polishing their resume. Employees want to make a valued-added contribution.

Organizations have the power and obligation to place people in jobs where they can add the most value.

Sometimes the reality of frantic production schedules and deadlines reduces the involvement of the employees in the debate and deliberations about the future of the organization. Limiting employee involvement in the decision-making process also diminishes the level of discretionary effort.

Another way the leadership team dampens the discretionary effort of employees is by following the mantra "Get it done, no matter what you need to do," and ignoring the hitches, glitches, and snags. Leaders with this operating mode only put a bandage on problems. The bandage is no substitute for tackling the real problem by blocking out the necessary time, sitting down with employees, and making the appropriate efforts to solve systemic problems.

One organization, a hospital we worked with, had an explicit policy that negatives should never be shared with the patients. In the spirit of customer service, this policy might be seen as valid. However, the explicit policy matched an unhealthy implicit policy to likewise abstain from speaking about problems with management. The implicit policy worked like a brick wall to stop any progress in the facility. Ignoring systemic problems diminishes trust leading to less discretionary effort contributed by employees.

The leadership team has the obligation to build a culture that maximizes, not dilutes, the discretionary effort of employees. They must take the challenge of addressing systemic problems that discourage workers and personalizing their approach to each employee's career in a way that incentivizes and maximizes the desire to give discretionary effort.

Discretionary Effort Drivers

The benefits of discretionary effort are an outgrowth of leaders focusing on the elements of the job that are important to their employees and then learning how to tie these elements to achieving business goals and objectives. The employee then becomes directly engaged in the success of the organization. This book provides discretionary effort drivers leaders can implement:

- Providing clear vision and transparency
- Generating pride in the organization
- Offering the ability to advance in the organization either vertically or laterally
- Permitting a certain amount of freedom over daily work flow
- Ensuring job assignments that fit with their natural talents and abilities
- Providing opportunities for personal growth and learning
- Giving proper recognition, appreciation and thanks for contributions
- Delegating clear work objectives that integrates the job description and project goals
- Considering personal needs

Factors that discourage discretionary effort are:

- Poor organizational communication
- Unclear work objectives
- Meager benefits
- Unsafe work conditions
- Non-competitive compensation
- Unfriendly work environment where conflict is allowed to fester
- Management and supervision that does not seem to care personally about employees

The RossBrandau Leadership Model provides a path for creating your leadership philosophy and building an organizational culture so a majority of employees give their personal best every day as they come to work. Going back to Chapter 10, you will see observable signs of success that the model is working when employees demonstrate conforming to the rules of safety, relating, aligning, and then emotionally committing to the organization. As they move through the levels and become authentic contributors, they create value in the way they become subject matter experts and leaders.

Each leadership level is an essential part of the foundation that paves the way for employees to reach authentic contribution, thereby turning them into your competitive advantage as they increase the profitability and economic sustainability of the company.

The Practice of Discretionary Effort

Leadership of One Power Principle:
Become the leader people choose to follow by earning the gift of discretionary effort from employees.

Reflection

Becoming the leader people choose to follow begins in your daily life experiences. Be your leader and discover your own discretionary effort in all areas of your life. If you can't see discretionary effort, then you can't develop its potential in yourself or others. Also recognize and enhance the factors that invite discretionary effort from all those around you. As you focus your observations in the workplace, remember that your example is the starting point to release the potential in all levels of the organization.

Discretionary Effort Exercise

Earn the Gift

The exercise for this chapter is to discover the invisible acts of discretionary effort that you and others perform during the work day. Think of the phrase "Earn the gift," acknowledge all forms of discretionary effort, and the invisible acts will materialize.

You are not used to looking for discretionary effort gifts in the workplace, so as you walk through the office, observe what is happening in the interactions between workers. At first, you will probably not observe anything new, but just like looking at a piece of artwork, the more you concentrate and examine, the more details you will see.

For instance, on your walk through the office, you may see a group of employees in passionate discussion. Ordinarily you would pay no attention, but this time you stop to ask what is happening. Their zealous discussion may expose a problem you did not even know existed. You acknowledge their discovery and give them permission and authority to solve the problem. This rather simplified example shows the process by which the concept of discretionary effort takes life.

Discretionary Effort Practice Steps:

Step 1: Observe and Experience. In the course of your day, be mindful of the discretionary effort you give and look for the obscure ways others offer discretionary effort.

Step 2: Contemplate and Record. Maintain a record of your observations of the gifts of discretionary effort from yourself or others.

Step 3: Share, Learn and Model. After you have evaluated the following questions, share your insights and ask for input from a mentor, a friend, or a trusted advisor.

4. What personal breakthroughs did I have in discovering my personal gifts of discretionary effort and contributions to the work day? Did I have any breakdowns in personal discretionary effort and energy?
5. What breakthroughs or breakdowns did I observe about the gifts of discretionary effort of my colleagues, direct reports or team members in the workplace?
6. What is the relationship between performance and gifts of discretionary effort?
7. How will I model gifts of discretionary energy in the workplace? How will I assess if it works as a strategy for discretionary effort?
8. Did you in any way experience the discretionary energy within you? Did it fuel you, multiply it and take yourself to another level of performance?

Reference

Potentiality. (n.d.). In *Merriam-Webster.com*. Retrieved from
http://www.merriam-webster.com/dictionary/potentiality

CONCLUSION

Join the Worldwide Leadership Initiative

To be successful in the 21st century requires the organization to meet the challenges of reducing costs while still increasing resources. This paradox can be achieved through a previously unrecognized source that is already in your budget: the discretionary effort of every individual in the organization.

When the discretionary effort of many individuals is combined, it creates synergy and can be observed as solutions-oriented energy that adds value at each step in the process of providing a product or service to a customer. It is untapped potential as it exists naturally within the mind of every employee, waiting for an invitation to be released. When the invitation is extended, discretionary effort is released as an intentional, free-will choice by the employee. When the gift of discretionary effort is unwrapped, it is visible in the efficiency, focus, and quality of outputs. It does not deplete the energy of individuals, but it creates a vitality that is hard to duplicate by other means. It is the secret to doing more with less.

Understanding the RossBrandau Discretionary Effort Leadership Model is the first step to releasing the gift of discretionary effort available within your organization and adopting 21st century leadership principles. The second step is to implement the principles and create an environment where employees naturally unwrap their character gifts of creativity and productivity by adopting key concepts:

1. Becoming a human-led value organization recognizing the human dignity of each individual
2. Using the power of gratitude and thanking employees for their contributions
3. Encouraging every manager to invest in professional development and become the leader of one—they lead themselves first and display excellence for those around them

Having a leadership team that demonstrates authentic contribution will create a multiplier effect and help employees achieve emotional commitment and rational alignment, so they do the right thing, the next right thing, and do it in the right way. Ultimately, some employees will become authentic contributors who willingly release their discretionary effort to increase profitability and sustainability in a competitive environment where organizations must continually learn and adapt. With a closer connection to customers and the marketplace, the organization will be more viable and economically sustainable.

Implementing the five leadership levels and moving an organization to a culture of discretionary effort isn't a quick fix. It takes some time and energy to create new habits, but discretionary effort transforms the culture of your organization to an environment of candid, serious discussion and debate, and it creates win-win solutions. It is contagious, and the results of your discretionary effort leadership initiative will move employees from minimal effort to amazing contributions.

Below is a summary of behaviors you can observe at each level of implementation.

- **Leadership Level One, Safety and Security
OBSERVABLE BEHAVIOR: CONFORMING**
When employees conform to safety rules and regulations and know their company is serious about security, they have a feeling of well-being. They are free to observe processes and services, contemplate how they could be improved and give discretionary effort.

- **Leadership Level Two, Social Acceptance
OBSERVABLE BEHAVIOR: RELATING**
As managers show acceptance of each individual, team members interact with each other, build professional relationships and collaborate. Discretionary effort is manifest as they find innovative solutions to daily problems.

- **Leadership Level Three, Rational Alignment**
  OBSERVABLE BEHAVIORS: ALIGNING
  Ensuring that the purpose and goals of the
  organization are articulated at all levels of the
  organization, enables workers to align their daily
  work routines with the organizational focus.

- **Leadership Level Four, Emotional Commitment**
  OBSERVABLE BEHAVIORS: SUPPORTING
  One definition for integrating is to combine parts to
  produce a whole or a larger unit. That is what
  happens at this level. Many individual employees
  decide to stay and help it pursue greatness. They
  become loyal employees.

- **Leadership Level Five, Authentic Contribution**
  OBSEVABLE BEHAVIORS: LEADING
  Because they are subject matter experts,
  employees who reach this level of contribution lead
  other employees regardless of their place on the
  organizational chart. They help create synergy of
  ideas to innovate.

The 21st century worldwide leadership initiative begins with each
manager choosing to practice discretionary effort and modeling it
through personal leadership, or the Leadership of One as we have
called it in this book. As each manager practices the principles and
employees follow their example, the more the value of
discretionary effort will be evident.

Join the Worldwide Discretionary Effort Leadership Initiative

You can join the worldwide discretionary effort initiative to transform your company into a 21st century workplace culture where discretionary effort is given on a regular basis by visiting www.DiscretionaryEffortLeadership.com. There you will find videos and podcasts for download and information on how to bring a Discretionary Effort Leadership program to your company.

We offer Power Triad coaching, public workshops and in-house programs to assist you in the implementation of discretionary effort leadership. View all options at www.DiscretionaryEffortLeadership.com.

If your company's level of engagement and contribution has plateaued, discretionary effort leadership can help put you on the upward path again. To assist you, this book is available for bulk sale at discounted prices to enable the learning and professional growth for every manager in your company.

Contact us:

Atlanta, Georgia Office
Karla Brandau, CEO
Workplace Power Institute
770-923-0883
Karla@KarlaBrandau.com
Karla.Brandau@DiscretionaryEffortLeadership.com

Toronto, Canada Office
Douglas Ross, CEO
Principle Dynamics
519-807-4132
PrincipleDynamics@gmail.com
Douglas.Ross@DiscretionaryEffortLeadership.com

About the Authors

Meet Karla Brandau

As CEO of Workplace Power Institute, Karla Brandau is an internationally known corporate trainer, consultant, keynote speaker, and executive coach. She has developed a depth and breadth of programs and keynotes that mark a clear path to leadership excellence and organizational success. She challenges leaders to proactively remove organizational obstacles to productivity and employee engagement, implementing the strategies outlined in *Discretionary Effort Leadership*.

Her client list includes many of the top-tiered Fortune 100 such as IBM, Coca Cola, Siemens, Chick-fil-A, as well as government agencies, nonprofits, and associations. She is a sought after industry thought-leader who speaks at both local and national conventions. To her credit, over 85 percent of the organizations who hire Karla, invite her back for repeat engagements.

As the consummate professional who listens and designs customized programs to meet company needs, she has delivered workshops to teach leadership principles, build teamwork, improve communication, develop creativity, and increase personal and team productivity. She is certified to deliver a variety of assessments and is widely known for her ability to administer and debrief personality profiles.

She is a media pro and has appeared on numerous television and radio business programs such as CNN, "Georgia Business Today," "Business Issues" with Alf Nucifora, Sirius XM, "A Woman's Place" on the AIBTV Network, and "MediaOne Spotlight" on MediaOne Cable News. She is a regular blogger, guest blogger, and newsletter and article writer.

The depth of her certifications and experience uniquely position her to help organizations implement the strategies outlined in *Discretionary Effort Leadership*. She is a Certified Speaking Professional (CSP), the National Speakers Association's international award for top professional platform competence and high earners. She is a Registered Corporate Coach (RCC) through the Worldwide Association of Business Coaches, a Certified Professional Behaviors Analyst (CPBA) having completed DISC behavioral analysis training, a Certified Professional Motivators Analyst (CPMA) having completed the Motivators training and a Certified Facilitator (CF). She graduated cum laude from Brigham Young University with a Bachelors of Arts degree in education.

Meet Douglas Ross

Douglas Ross is a senior manufacturing professional with extensive experience in product launches, cultural transformation, and plant turnaround involving lean operations and leadership development. He has worked in some of the world's most globally competitive industries and organizations including General Motors, Textron, Lennox, Rockwell, and DuPont.

He is often referred to as the consultant of last resort, the person brought in to resolve the impossible, solve the unsolvable workplace problems.

Doug was hired as a consultant to help turn around the St. Catherine General Motors (GM) component plant, which within 16 months went from twenty-eighth to third in performance output in their section, winning the Beat Toyota Award. In another GM contract, he helped the company set a record with a three-month Cadillac engine product launch that ultimately beat Toyota in a quality assessment. The two GM projects involved working with management, engineering, and between 1500 and 2000 unionized employees to achieve these exceptional results.

As a senior cultural change subject matter expert, he has led numerous organizations through cultural transformation and performance improvement. He has worked extensively with high level executives one-on-one in leadership development. Doug is a thought-leader and curriculum developer who field tests and implements leadership models and workplace strategies through consulting and executive coaching. He has worked with some of the world's most noted authorities on integrity and has developed and field-tested curriculum on integrity, discretionary effort, and other leadership related topics.

He worked jointly with Joseph Mondello, of New York, to develop a coaching program targeting the economically deprived young men and women of the world who cannot get jobs. The program combines 20th and 21st century employment techniques to help under-served youth. The program is currently being hosted by Helen Walker Adams, radio-TV show host, of Augusta, Georgia.

Doug holds a Master's degree and has completed doctorate course work in organizational development. He is also an experienced facilitator, an accomplished mediator, and a seminar leader in the area of cultural change and performance improvement. His past employment includes experience as a college professor, college administrator, and a human resources director.

Made in the USA
Columbia, SC
08 July 2018